JONAH
AND
NAHUM

JONAH
AND
NAHUM

by
John R. Kohlenberger III

MOODY PRESS
CHICAGO

Except where noted, Scripture taken from the *Holy Bible: New International Version.* Copyright © 1973, 1978 by the International Bible Society. Used by permission of Zondervan Bible Publishers.

The proper name of God, rendered as "Lord" in all modern versions except the *Jerusalem Bible,* is referred to in this commentary as "Yahweh" in text and translation.

English Versions of the Bible

JB   *Jerusalem Bible*
KJV   King James Version (Authorized Version)
LB   *Living Bible*
NASB *New American Standard Bible*
NEB   *New English Bible*
NIV   *New International Version*
NJV   New Jewish Version (The Torah, The Prophets, The Writings)
NKJV *New King James Version*
RSV   Revised Standard Version
TEV   *Today's English Version* (Good News Bible)

Library of Congress Cataloging in Publication Data

Kohlenberger III, John R.
  Jonah and Nahum

  (Everyman's Bible commentary)
  Bibliography: p.
  1. Bible. O.T. Jonah—Commentaries. 2. Bible.
O.T. Nahum—Commentaries. I. Title. II. Series.
BS1605.3.I64 1984   224'.92   84-1153
ISBN 0-8024-0352-2

1 2 3 4 5 6 7 Printing/LC/Year 88 87 86 85 84

Printed in the United States of America

CONTENTS

To Edward W. Goodrick
Teacher, Mentor, Colleague, Friend

PREFACE

The public sees only the author's name on a book, but must never deduce from this that he or she produced it alone. I would like to thank a few of the many who made this volume possible.

Though he is no longer with Moody Press, I wish to thank Chuck Phelps for originally introducing me to Moody, and Phil Rawley for the invitation to contribute this volume to the series. I must thank Garry Knussman, and the Press, for their patience as I missed deadline after deadline, and Steven Cory for his swift editing of the manuscript. I also wish to thank the people at the Zondervan Corporation for their gracious permission to quote extensively from the *New International Version*.

I must thank my wife, Carolyn, and children, Sarah and Joshua, for their encouragement and for reminding me that I am a husband and father before I am a researcher and writer.

Though so many have contributed to my educational development, I must single out Dave Needham of Multnomah School of the Bible, who first opened my eyes to the message and heart of the prophets, and Bob Hughes of Western Conservative Baptist Seminary, who further developed for me the great theological themes of the prophets and provided me with a great outline of Jonah.

But of all my teachers, I must especially acknowledge Ed Goodrick. Our relation began as teacher and student, grew to mentor and disciple, and continues as colleagues and co-writers. His love for God and His word and his standards of excellence in pursuing the knowledge of the Holy have given me a model for life. To him this little volume is affectionately dedicated.

GENERAL INTRODUCTION

GENERAL CONSIDERATIONS

Jonah and Nahum are the fifth and seventh books of the section of the Scriptures popularly known as the "Minor Prophets." This label distinguishes the twelve small books of this section (known, by the way, as "The Twelve" in the Hebrew Bible) from the four larger "Major Prophets." Calling these books "Minor," because of their relative size, should not distract us from the major significance of their messages.

Besides sharing a place in the same section of canon, these books also have in common their uniqueness in relation to the other prophets. Jonah is primarily a narrative, where the other prophets are primarily proclamations. Nahum is a dirge, a song celebrating the downfall of a foreign kingdom, with hardly a word directed toward Israel or Judah, as is normal with the other prophets.

Jonah is certainly the best known of the prophets, whereas many Christians (perhaps most) do not have the faintest idea of what the book of Nahum is about. More will be said about these two unusual, but valuable books in their special introductions.

PROPHETS AND PROPHECY

WHAT IS A PROPHET?

Because of the explosion of books on "prophecy" in the seventies, many Christians (and non-Christians) have the wrong idea about the role of the prophet and the function of prophecy. Contrary to the emphasis of popular paperbacks, biblical prophets were not primarily *foretellers,* predictors of the future; they were *forth-tellers,* preachers of God's word.

Exodus 7:1-2 provides a graphic illustration of the role of the prophet, seen in the relationship between Moses and Aaron. Because Moses had complained of his inability properly or eloquently to proclaim God's word to Pharaoh, God brought in Aaron to act as a prophet, while Moses would be "like God" to Pharaoh. Moses was the *source* of the message, Aaron, the prophet, was the *speaker.*

PROPHECY: PROCLAMATION AND PREDICTION

As to the function of prophecy, Moses again serves as a fine example. The largest portion of God's revelation through Moses was the law. This body of revelation was not, as many Christians have unfortunately misunderstood it, a code of legalistic regulations, but was the key to life under the Old Covenant. Every Israelite, as every believer of all time, was called into right relation with God by love and faith (Deut. 6:4-5). This relationship was worked out by following God's will as revealed in His Word (Deut. 6:6-9), as is true of Christians today (John 14:15; 1 John 5:2-3). In fact, the Hebrew word *torah* literally means "instruction" or "pointing the way," though this meaning is not seen in the word "law," which normally translates it. So, far from being simply legislation, the law pointed the way to successful life in relation to God and His creation.

Most of the law related to the present, to everyday life. However, it was prophecy, and Moses is called a prophet (Deut. 18:15, 18; 34:10). The predictive element of the law—what people usually think of as prophecy—was used to reinforce the commands and principles by declaring what the future held for those who responded or failed to respond (e.g., Deut. 28—29).

Another dimension of the predictive element of prophecy appears when God declares what He will do in the course of immediate history, as with the ten plagues on Egypt in Exodus 7—12. But these predictions do not function simply to show off God's knowledge of the future, or to excite human curiosity, but to reinforce other revelation. In this case, the other revelation is the *action* of God. The predictions declare what God will do, the actions reveal His character, and the explanation that follows amplifies on and applies the message. See, for example, the prediction of God's victory over Pharaoh at the Red Sea in Exodus 14:1-4, 15-18; the fulfilling event in 14:19-29; and the explanations and applications in 14:30-31; 15:1-21; Psalm 144; and Habakkuk 3.

Thus, though prophecy does have a predictive element, that is secondary to its primary function of revealing and applying the will of God to the people of God.

MODES OF PROPHECY

God spoke "at many times and in various ways" to His prophets (Heb. 1:1). Moses further illustrates these *modes* of communication. God communicated to him audibly (Ex. 3:1—4:17) and even in writing (Ex. 32:15-16). He spoke to him face to face, though He usually addressed His prophets in visions, dreams, and riddles (Num. 12:6-8; cf. Amos 7:1-9; 8:1-2). As mentioned above, God also revealed Himself in actions.

The prophet, then, usually received the word of God in some sort of visionary state. Thus, two of the three Hebrew words normally used to describe the prophet (*rō'eh* [2095b] and *ḥōzeh* [633b][1]) are translated "seer," apparently emphasizing the reception of God's word. The usual word for prophet (*nābî'* [1277a]), though sometimes synonymous with the others (e.g., 1 Sam. 9:9; 2 Sam. 24:11), apparently emphasized the prophet's function as an authorized spokesman of God's word.

1. The numbers that follow Hebrew words cited throughout this book refer to the numbering system in the fine *Theological Wordbook of the Old Testament* (Chicago: Moody, 1980). Those desiring more detailed historical and theological word studies will be greatly helped by this set.

Moses presented the word of God primarily in verbal form, at times proclaiming the word he had heard (Ex. 24:3) and at other times reading the word that had been written down (Ex. 24:7). The book of Deuteronomy is a sermon, an address given on a single occasion, based on the previously written word of God and applied to the particular needs of the group of Israelites who would enter and conquer the land of promise. Moses also communicated the word of God in writing, not just recording dictation as a scribe (which he did do, Ex. 24:4) but also in revealing God's interaction with and perspective on human history, as in Leviticus 10; 24:10-23.

The prophets who followed Moses usually proclaimed the word of God after the fashion of Deuteronomy, interweaving the revealed law and past history with a contemporary perspective and fresh revelation.[2] Sometimes, they acted out this communication as living parables (Ezek. 4—5; cf. Isa. 8:18). Again, the predictive elements of their prophecies were primarily warnings and promises to those who accepted or rejected God's word at the time of the prophecy (Hos. 13:9).

With this perspective, we can better understand why the books of Joshua, Judges, Samuel, and Kings are considered the "Former Prophets" in the Hebrew canon. Not only are they traditionally understood as having been written by prophets, but they also give a prophetic perspective on Israel's history, showing the coincidence of the ups (blessings) and downs (curses) to obedience and disobedience to the law (2 Kings 17:7-23, especially verse 13; 22:1-20). We can also better understand why the book of Jonah would be considered a book of prophecy, when the sum total of its prophetic utterance is only five Hebrew words (3:4)!

---

2. Interestingly, both Jonah and Nahum base the thrust of their messages on the same text: Exodus 34:6-7. However, Jonah emphasizes the forgiving aspect of God's longsuffering (Ex. 34:6 in Jonah 4:2), whereas Nahum emphasizes the judgment to come at the end of God's longsuffering (Ex. 34:7 in Nah. 1:3). The significance of this text to both prophets is discussed in more detail in the commentary and the appendix.

JONAH

JONAH: INTRODUCTION

When dealing with the introduction to or background of a book of the Bible, one normally seeks to define and understand the writer(s), the intended audience; the book's place of origin and destination; its date, purpose, message, and literary form; as well as problems related to text, historicity, and canonicity. Unfortunately, with the book of Jonah we are short on concrete information and long on opinion, controversy, and problems.

Our task is further complicated by the familiarity of the basic story of Jonah, which makes it difficult to propose new insights or approaches to the book, and by the fact that historically, conservative interpreters have been almost unanimous in their approach to and understanding of Jonah, and have been diametrically opposed to the methods and interpretations of non-conservatives.

However, in expending so much time defending and even trying to prove that the amazing and miraculous events of the book actually happened, most conservatives have missed the tremendous theological and practical insights that many liberals have proposed from their critical studies. This volume is written from a conservative perspective, believing the events of Jonah to have occurred just as the text states they did; but it borrows from any and all sources that grapple with the meaning and application of the text, regardless of their perspective. The annotated bibliography at the end of the commentary will apply the appropriate labels to these sources for those who wish to do further, discerning research.

Purpose and Date

The purpose and date of the book of Jonah are closely related. Virtually all interpreters agree that the *events* of the book are claimed to have occurred in the days of Jeroboam II of Israel (who reigned from 793 to 753 B.C.), whether or not they believe the events actually occurred. However, there are no direct statements in the text that demand that the book was *written* during this era. The purpose of the book helps determine the date of composition.

Jonah clearly and dramatically portrays God as Yahweh,[1] the Creator of all things (1:9, 17; 4:6-8) and the Savior of all people (1:15-16; 2:6, 9; 3:10), not just Israel. Further, the book explains the conditional nature of prophecy: God can and does change His mind when people change their ways (3:10; 4:2).

Many commentators have argued that Jonah typifies the devout Jew of his era.[2] If this is so, his (1) strong desire to keep knowledge of salvation from the nations because he knows Yahweh will save them if they repent (4:2), and his (2) own failure to repent in light of his knowledge of God highlight the need the book's audience has to change its thinking and action in relation to God and the nations.

When both of these thrusts are considered, the era of Jeroboam II does indeed form a suitable setting. The prophets Hosea and Amos fiercely denounced the Northern Kingdom for its complacent materialism, its abuse of the poor, and its idolatry with a message of impending judgment. Jonah added to this a message of Yahweh's love for the nations, countering whatever eliteness or security Israel might think to have as God's elect, and also offered a way of escape

---

1. The proper name of God, rendered as "Lord" in all modern versions except the *Jerusalem Bible,* is referred to in this commentary as "Yahweh" in text and translation. See TWOT pp. 210-12 for more information on pronunciation and translation.
2. Brevard S. Childs, *Introduction to the Old Testament as Scripture,* pp. 424-25.

from impending judgment: repentance. Jonah's predecessors, Elijah and Elisha, had also demonstrated Yahweh's love for the nations in the previous century (1 Kings 17:7-24; 2 Kings 5).

Conservatives, then, have traditionally dated Jonah around 760 B.C., immediately preceding Amos and Hosea. More recently, liberal scholars have opted for a post-exilic date of around 430 B.C. or later. This date is based on the interpretation that sees Jonah as a universalistic message of Yahweh's love for all peoples, specifically opposed to the "narrow exclusivism" of the days of Ezra and Nehemiah.[3] This position is further strengthened by many other details, some of the major ones including:

1. The phrase "king of Nineveh" (3:6) and the apparently exaggerated size of the city (3:3) seem to indicate Nineveh (which fell in 612 B.C.) as distant memory.
2. Reflection of Persian customs (having animals mourn, in 3:8) rather than Assyrian customs.
3. Apparent use of Jeremiah 18:7-8 and Joel 2:13-14 (as the basis of chapters 3-4).
4. Use of "post-exilic" Aramaic and Hebrew vocabulary.[4]

Though many liberals now admit that the dating of Jonah in the days of Ezra and Nehemiah cannot be based on its message,[5] most are still persuaded by the weight of the other details. However, many liberal and most conservative writers have solid counters to these arguments, which are well summarized by Landes and Archer:[6]

1. Neither the use of the title "king of Nineveh" nor the repentance of the animals are necessarily contrary to Assyrian custom.

3. W. Neil, "Jonah, Book of," 2.964.
4. Leslie C. Allen, *The Books of Joel, Obadiah, Jonah and Micah,* pp. 186-88.
5. Gerhard von Rad, *Old Testament Theology* 2:292.
6. G. M. Landes, "Jonah, Book of," 5:490; Gleason L. Archer, *A Survey of Old Testament Introduction,* pp. 309-13.

2. The size of Nineveh is not an absolute description, but refers to the amount of time Jonah would need to work his way through the city and its environs.
3. Jonah certainly shares the theological emphases of Jeremiah 18 and Joel 2, but all three can be derived from earlier sources, especially Exodus 32—34.
4. The vocabulary is most probably influenced by Phoenician, and thus dates from before the Exile.
5. The message of Jonah, that God would change His mind concerning judgment if the people repented, would seem to lose a lot of its punch after the fall of Israel (722 B.C.), Nineveh (612 B.C.), and Judah (586 B.C.).

HISTORICITY

With few exceptions,[7] the book of Jonah has been treated as genuine history until recently. Most who reject the historicity of Jonah do so because of the miraculous element, not because any of the previously mentioned problems are so compelling. However, the miraculous frequently plays a part in prophetic narrative (as in the Elijah and Elisha stories mentioned earlier), and serves in Jonah to highlight Yahweh's intense involvement with His creation:

1. The stilling of the storm convinces the sailors of who Yahweh is, resulting in their salvation (1:15-16).
2. The great fish saves Jonah from drowning and returns him to land to continue his mission (1:17—2:10).
3. The mass repentance of Nineveh results in their salvation (3:10) and also in teaching Jonah.
4. The plant, the worm, and the wind (4:6-8) complete the narrative and Jonah's education.

Many who reject the historicity of Jonah agree that the miraculous element is a didactic device to help bring home the

7. Allen, pp. 178-79.

message, but read the book not as history but as a parable.[8] However, parables must reflect real life in order to bring home the message. "This means that, if the miraculous will not do in history, it equally will lend no conviction to a parable."[9]

Most conservative writers believe that Jesus' use of Jonah in His preaching (Matt. 12:39-41; 16:4; Luke 11:29-32) is conclusive evidence for the book's historicity, though others believe this argument is not convincing.[10] So, given that God can and does perform the miraculous, and in light of the history of interpretation, including Jesus' use of Jonah, the book should be considered historically accurate.

LITERARY FORM

That Jonah is historically accurate does not mean that the book is simply a chronicle of events or a biography, as it is so often interpreted by conservatives. Rather, the repetitive vocabulary, the lack of historical details, and the balanced structure give the impression that Jonah is a parable-like composition. Jesus' use of Jonah as typical of His own preaching and impending resurrection, and His reference to the Ninevites as typical of repentance (Matt. 12:39-41; Luke 11:29-32) might further demonstrate the parabolic nature of the book.

Many, however, have pushed the symbolism of Jonah too far, making it into a full-blown allegory. Because Jonah means "dove" in Hebrew, and "dove" is used in Hosea 11:11 and Psalm 74:19 as a metaphor for Israel, then Jonah must mean Israel. The fish symbolizes the Babylonian exile, and so forth. But for as many symbols as these interpreters locate, others elude their grasp.[11]

A more controlled parabolic interpretation, however,

8. Julius A. Bewer, "A Commentary on Jonah," pp. 3-4.
9. D. W. B. Robinson, "Jonah," p. 746.
10. Archer, p. 313; Allen, p. 180.
11. Michael C. Griffiths, "Jonah," p. 978; Archer, pp. 308-9.

allows Jonah to be genuine history and yet represent realities beyond the specific designations of the text.

We have already seen Jesus using Jonah for direct application to His setting; but this could not have been understood by Jonah's original audience. Rather, they would have seen Jonah as representing the devout Jew, a man well-versed in the law (4:2) and hymns (2:2-9) of Israel. Yet for all his knowledge of Yahweh, he refused to be a channel of blessing to all nations (Gen. 12:3).

The sailors and the Ninevites would then represent the nations, lost in their ignorant idolatry (1:5; 4:11) yet ready to respond to the God of Israel (1:15; 3:10). Their ready repentance demonstrated to Israel that Yahweh's love reaches all nations (cf. Amos 9:11-12; Acts 11:18), and pointed out to Israel her need to repent of her hardness to Yahweh and her aloofness from the nations.

JONAH THE MAN

In the Old Testament Jonah is mentioned only in 2 Kings 14:25 and in the book that bears his name. In the New Testament he is mentioned only in regard to "the sign of Jonah" in Matthew 12:39-41; 16:4, and Luke 11:29-32.

Because Jonah was born in Gath-Hepher, a town on the border of Zebulun and Naphtali (Jos. 19:13) near Nazareth, and because he prophesied about the military and material successes of Jeroboam II, he is considered a prophet to the Northern Kingdom. But unlike the typical northern prophet of this era (1 Kings 22:1-28; Amos 7:10-17), Jonah actually worshiped Yahweh (1:9) and sought Him in His Temple (2:4).

Jonah is a figure of paradox. Though he worshiped Yahweh, he fled from His service (1:3, 10). He prayed that Yahweh would save him from death at sea (2:2-9), yet prayed to Yahweh to take his life after Nineveh repented (4:3, 8). After joyfully praising Yahweh for His gracious salvation of Jonah (2:2-9), he angrily criticized Yahweh for His compassionate salvation of Nineveh (4:1-2). And though his message ef-

fected the repentance and salvation of the Gentiles he con-
tacted (1:9-16; 3:4-10), his own knowledge of the law (4:2)
and hymnody (2:2-9) of Israel did not effect his own repentance.

Jonah was not schizophrenic. But he did have tunnel vision. He clearly saw the compassionate grace of Yahweh
when it was extended to His covenant people Israel, but could
not share Yahweh's vision for the rest of the world. Jonah's
attitude reminds me of so many Christians whose "theology
is clear as ice—and twice as cold!" (to quote Mickey Day, one
of my former theology teachers).

We do not read of Jonah's repentance and restoration at
the end of the book. But we hope that because the book was
written, and because its message of Yahweh's desire for both
Israel and the nations is so clear, that Jonah did eventually
come around. At least we have the opportunity to learn from
Jonah's mistakes and share Yahweh's desire for our total sub-
mission to His will, and for the salvation and acceptance of
all people, regardless of how attractive or unattractive they
may be to us.

THE SIGN OF JONAH

"The sign of Jonah" is mentioned in Matthew 12:39; 16:4,
and Luke 11:29-32. Matthew specifies (12:40) that Jonah's
three days and three nights in the belly of the fish will parallel
Jesus' three days and three nights in the heart of the earth.
Thus for many readers "the sign of Jonah" is the type or
prophecy of the resurrection. Luke, however, does not make
this connection. He states that "as Jonah was a sign to the
Ninevites, so also will the Son of Man be to this generation"
(Luke 11:30).

Many interpreters take Luke's account as genuinely reflect-
ing the words of Christ, but see Matthew's as an interpretation to provide Old Testament background for the resurrection. In this scheme, "the sign of Jonah" is simply the
preaching of repentance, which is all that Jesus will offer to

His generation.[12] Luke, however, refers to Jesus as a *future* sign ("will be"), thus at least leaving open the possibility of His referring to the resurrection, in harmony with Matthew.

But how was Jonah a sign to the Ninevites? John Walton deduces from what is known of the theology of the Ninevites that Jonah was the finale in a series of signs.[13] The timing of his visit and the content of his preaching pointed the Ninevites to the need to repent and accept his God. That they could read these signs is in direct contrast to the Pharisees and Sadducees, who demanded a sign from Jesus but could not "interpret the signs of the times" (Matt. 16:3).

Perhaps the mention of Solomon in both Matthew 12 and Luke 11 aids our understanding. The Queen of Sheba's positive response to Solomon's wisdom (1 Kings 10:1-13; 2 Chron. 9:1-12) rebukes the Pharisees and scribes, as does the Ninevites' repentance at the preaching of Jonah. Both men had in common a message and the evidence of the activity of Yahweh in their lives. The queen was as impressed by Solomon's wealth as by his wisdom, and praised Yahweh for giving both to him. The sailors of Jonah 1 were moved to worship Yahweh after both hearing Jonah's words and seeing the actions of Yahweh in bringing and stilling the storm. Perhaps the pattern of the sailors in Jonah 1 and the Queen of Sheba in Matthew and Luke allows us to deduce that the Ninevites believed God because of Jonah's preaching *and* because of the sign of his salvation from the sea by the fish and/or the timing of his visit.

Matthew specifically mentions the salvation of Jonah from the fish in relation to the sign, but also refers to Jonah's preaching. Luke specifically mentions Jonah's preaching, but also implies his salvation from the fish. "The sign of Jonah" then might best be interpreted as "the authorisation of the

12. Bewer, p. 10.
13. John Walton, *Jonah*, pp. 77-79.

divine messenger by deliverance from death.''[14] The sign is not just the resurrection; nor is it just the preaching of repentance. God validates His messengers and their message by miraculous intervention in their lives.

Jonah, then, displays a general pattern of God's activity in verifying the message of His representatives, very much in line with the guidelines for prophets (Deut. 18:21-22) and the example of Solomon. And though Jonah did not exist simply to be a type of Christ, Matthew is fully justified in comparing the details of Yahweh's salvation of Jonah to the resurrection of Jesus, not only because of the remarkable coincidence of the time span, but also because of the parallel of location: "the *belly* of a huge fish" and "the *heart* of the earth" (Matt. 12:40).

THE MESSAGE OF JONAH FOR TODAY

The two major messages of Jonah are still for today and are intertwined: God is *sovereign*; and God is *Savior*. God desired to save the Ninevites from their sin, and commissioned Jonah to preach to them. Though Jonah ran away, God used His creation to bring Jonah back, and in the process saved the sailors from their sin—while also saving them and Jonah from death at sea.

But all of the events of the book seem to be directed to the end of saving Jonah from his wrong thinking and actions toward Yahweh and toward the Ninevites. For though he did obey Yahweh and did preach in Nineveh, he never repented of the attitude that sent him into disobedience in the first place.

Thus, though Yahweh displayed His sovereignty in the storm and in stilling the storm, which resulted in the sailors' physical and spiritual salvation; and though He changed his mind about bringing destruction on Nineveh, also resulting in

---

14. Gerhard Kittel and Gerhard Friedrich, eds., *Theological Dictionary of the New Testament* 3:409. (Article by Joachim Jeremias.)

their physical and spiritual salvation; we read only of Jonah's physical salvation from drowning. The spiritual (or attitudinal) salvation for which Yahweh sent the plant, the worm, and the wind is not realized in the narrative. The book is as open-ended with regard to Jonah. It awaits his application of its message to himself, as it awaits our application of its message today.

This open-endedness serves to highlight further the attribute of Yahweh that underlies His sovereignty and saving: His slowness to anger or, in more traditional language, "longsuffering." That Yahweh is longsuffering means He endures and holds back judgment on sin in order to give sinners time to respond.

Longsuffering is *gracious* in that those who do respond rightly are saved. In Jonah the gracious side of Yahweh's longsuffering is seen, resulting in the salvation of the sailors and the Ninevites, and in the potential salvation of Jonah. However, longsuffering is also *judgmental* in that those who do not respond have added to their sin, and thus have greatly increased their judgment. Interestingly, in Nahum this judgmental side of longsuffering is seen, resulting in the ultimate destruction of unrepentant Nineveh. (This concept is further developed in the appendix.)

In Jonah's day the message was to a self-centered, affluent Israel, bent on personal peace and prosperity at the expense of the physical well-being of her own countrymen and the spiritual well-being of the nations, and at the expense of right relation to Yahweh. The self-centered, affluent church in America today is in the same situation as Israel of two and a half millennia ago. We need individually and corporately to examine our lives and ministries, to see where we are failing in ministering to the needy both within the Body and in the world, and in our relation to our Lord and King.

As Jonah chronicled the result of the repentance of the nations, Joel wrote of what could happen following the repentance of God's covenant people:

Who knows but that he may turn and have pity
  and leave behind a blessing—
grain offerings and drink offerings
  for Yahweh your God.

(Joel 2:14)

In other words, if we respond rightly to Yahweh's plan for us, He enlarges our capability to fulfill that plan, bringing us joy and satisfaction, but especially bringing Him glory and honor.

OUTLINE

This "chiastic" outline shows the basic parallel structure of the book.

A1. Yahweh's Longsuffering Toward Jonah, 1:1—2:10.
  B1. Jonah's Unexplained Disobedience, 1:1-3.
    C1. Yahweh Saves the Sailors, 1:4-16.
      D1. Yahweh Saves Jonah, 1:17—2:10.
    C2. Yahweh Saves Nineveh, 3:1-10.
  B2. Jonah's Disobedience Explained and Challenged, 4:1-11.
A2. Yahweh's Longsuffering Toward Nineveh, 3:1—4:11.

Notice that the progression of the book works toward the middle and then doubles back on itself. This form is called "chiasm," and serves to highlight the central event or statement. The center of the book of Jonah is the event of Yahweh saving Jonah and Jonah's statement, "Salvation comes from Yahweh" (2:9).

This use of chiasm is a conscious literary device used throughout the Bible, especially in Hebrew poetry. Its simplest form involves two parallel lines, with the beginning of the first line matching the content of the end of the second line and vice versa, as in Psalm 1:6:

For Yahweh watches over / the way of the righteous,
but the way of the wicked / will perish.

When these lines are set side by side, you connect the parallel parts with an "X," or Greek *chi,* thus "*chi*asm." When outlined as the book of Jonah above, the parallel members become more obvious:

    a1. For Yahweh watches over
        b1. the way of the righteous,
        b2. but the way of the wicked
    a2. will perish.

By setting the two "ways" next to each other, the psalmist especially emphasizes their contrast, which is the key to the whole psalm.

Narratives, too, can use chiastic construction to emphasize crucial points. Jonah 1:4-16 is a carefully constructed episode that begins, ends, and centers on the "fear of Yahweh" (see its outline). But even 1:3 is a chiasm in the Hebrew:

But Jonah got up
    to flee to *Tarshish* from the presence of Yahweh
        and he *went down* to Joppa
            and he found a ship
                going to *Tarshish*
            so he paid its fare
        and he *went down* into it
    to go with them to *Tarshish* from the presence of Yah-
    weh.

By chiastic construction, the writer emphasizes where Jonah is going, "to Tarshish" (beginning, end, middle), and that this journey is "down," while Yahweh is "up" (1:2). The repetitions of language and the symmetry of construction reinforce the point of Jonah's disobedience and leave a memorable, esthetic impression of *sovereign* design in the historical events. For as the writer crafted the narration for the observant reader, Yahweh had crafted the events for Jonah.[15]

15. For more on parallelism and chiasm in Jonah, see Allen, pp. 197-99, 204, and G. M. Landes, "The Kerygma of the Book of Jonah." On chiasm in general, see Nils W. Lund, *Chiasms in the New Testament* (Chapel Hill, N.C.: U. of North Carolina, 1942).

1

JONAH'S UNEXPLAINED DISOBEDIENCE; YAHWEH SAVES THE SAILORS

(JONAH 1:1-16)

JONAH'S UNEXPLAINED DISOBEDIENCE (1:1-3)

GOD CALLS (1)

The book of Jonah begins just like any of the other prophetic books. But that which follows the introductory formula is unique in biblical literature.

The introduction "The word of Yahweh came to . . .", in similar form, appears at the beginning of nine of the other fifteen prophets (Jer. 1:2; Ezek. 1:3; Hos. 1:1; Joel 1:1; Mic. 1:1; Zeph. 1:1; Hag. 1:1; Zech. 1:1; Mal. 1:1). Usually the revelatory communication is a message that the prophet must proclaim to its intended audience (Jer. 2:1—3:5); sometimes the word is the prophet's call to service (Jer. 1:4-19). At other times (Hos. 1:1—3:5), the word is specific instruction for the prophet himself, as is the case in Jonah.

In all of the other instances in Scripture, the prophets responded accordingly. What God commanded to proclaim, they proclaimed. When the Sovereign called, they answered. When Yahweh instructed, they obeyed. Not so Jonah! Yahweh says, Go east, but Jonah heads west!

THE FIRST COMMISSION (2)

Yahweh commissioned Jonah to go to Nineveh and "preach against it." This is the first of many surprises in the book. For though every prophet had something to say about the nations, none of them was ever sent outside the safety of his own country with the message! True, Elijah was sent among the nations (e.g., 1 Kings 17:8; 19:15), but not with a message of judgment. Daniel prophesied in Babylon, but did not cry out in the streets against the populace.

The first thing we hear about the city is its size, its greatness (cf. Gen. 10:11-12), for it was with Asshur and Calah one of the principal cities of the massive Assyrian empire. (See 3:3 for additional material on Nineveh.) Reiterated three times in the book (3:1, 2; 4:11), this description may conjure up thoughts of great wickedness and cruelty (cf. "Babylon the Great," Rev. 14:8). However, its main use in 4:11 is to emphasize how many people are in need of Yahweh's forgiveness, how many would perish in their ignorance without knowledge of God.

Jonah was to "preach against" Nineveh ("proclaim judgment," NJV) because of her "wickedness" ($r\bar{a}'\hat{a}$ [2191c]). This significant word and its cognates appear ten times in Jonah (1:7, 8; 3:8, 10 [2x]; 4:1[2x], 2, 6), in fascinating word plays. That which is "wicked" or "evil" to God is absolute wrong (1:2; 3:8, 10*a*). But the actions of *God* are also referred to by this label! The "destruction" (3:10*b*) or "calamity" (4:2) God threatened on Nineveh was evil from the residents' perspective. Ironically, so was God's compassion, which "greatly displeased" Jonah (4:1).

JONAH DISOBEYS (3)

The second surprise of the book, much greater than the first, is that "Jonah ran away from Yahweh"! Elijah had run away from Jezebel and complained about his situation to God (1 Kings 19:3-18). Jeremiah (20:9) had unsuccessfully tried to keep from proclaiming the word of Yahweh. But Jonah's blatant rebellion is unparalleled.

Why did Jonah run? This is resolved in chapter 4, but certainly the original readers would have speculated upon their first encounter with the book. Fear of the Ninevites would be a clear possibility, for the Assyrians were famous for cruelty to their enemies (Nah. 3:1, 19). Many suggest that since Jonah was being sent to Nineveh, rather than denouncing it from afar, God was giving the people the chance to repent and be forgiven.[1] This brings up two more possibilities. Jonah may have been afraid of being considered a false prophet if his oracle about Nineveh's destruction did not come to pass (Deut. 18:22). After all, he was famous for his fulfilled prediction of the successes of Jeroboam II (2 Kings 14:25). More likely, Jonah simply did not want Yahweh to *be* Yahweh, the gracious and compassionate God, to any other people than Israel. But this is jumping ahead of the narrative; more will be said at 4:2 and 11.

Where did Jonah run? Joppa, 33 miles west of Jerusalem, was the only natural harbor on Israel's Mediterranean coast. There Jonah could catch a ship, most likely Phoenician, to any western destination. Ironically, the city Jonah visited to escape his mission to the Gentiles was the city where Peter's vision would mark the beginning of the mission to the Gentiles in the New Covenant (Acts 10:9-23)!

"Tarshish" is usually identified with Tartessos (TEV) in southwest Spain.[2] In other biblical texts, it is a faraway commercial city of legendary wealth (Jer. 10:9; Ezek. 27:12, 25). But Isaiah (66:19) probably captures the sense in which Tarshish is used here, as a land so distant it has "not heard of my [Yahweh's] fame or seen [His] glory." The point is clear: Jonah's action is exactly opposite to Yahweh's command.

How could Jonah run away "from Yahweh" (1:3 [twice], 10)? The same Hebrew phrase is often used to describe items inside the tabernacle, "before Yahweh" (Lev. 10:2; 16:12; Num. 20:9), and of those in the presence of royalty (Gen. 41:46; 2 Kings 6:32). The picture could be that Jonah was

1. Michael C. Griffiths, "Jonah," p. 980.
2. Leslie C. Allen, *The Books of Joel, Obadiah, Jonah and Micah*, p. 204.

leaving an audience with Yahweh in the Temple.[3] For though Jonah was from Galilee and prophesied about the Northern Kingdom, he did "worship Yahweh" (1:9) and seek Him in His Temple (2:4, 7). One as familiar with the Psalms as Jonah (see comments on chapter 2) certainly did not think he could escape Yahweh (Ps. 139:7-8). Rather, he was formally leaving "the service" of Yahweh (NJV) by refusing to obey Him.

Notice that Jonah "went down" to Joppa, "went down" (NASB) into the ship, "went down" into its hold (1:5) and finally hit bottom when he "sank down" to the bottom of the sea (2:6). This careful repetition of vocabulary doubly emphasizes the wrong direction of Jonah's movements, for Yahweh is "up" in the metaphor of verse 2.

YAHWEH SAVES THE SAILORS (1:4-16)

The rest of chapter 1 parallels chapter 3, both of them speaking of Yahweh's compassion on and salvation of the Gentiles. They serve to frame chapter 2, in which Jonah himself is saved and thus proclaims in the very center of the book, "Salvation comes from Yahweh!" (2:9). This symmetrical, "chiastic" framework is pointed out in the Outline (see Introduction to Jonah).

Scholars have also noted that 1:4-16 is itself a carefully constructed chiasm.[4] The following outline displays the parallel elements and forms the basis of the comments:

3. John Walton, *Jonah*, p. 14.
4. Allen, p. 197.

a1. Narrative (Storm Begins) and Response of Fear, 4-5*b*.
  b1. Sailors' Prayer (each to his own god), 5*b*.
    c1. Narrative (Cargo Ejected; Jonah Sleeps), 5*c*-6*a*.
      d1. Captain's Command (Get up and pray!), 6*b*.
        e1. Sailors' Speech (Let's cast lots.), 7*a*.
          f1. Narrative (Lot Falls to Jonah), 7*b*.
            g1. Sailors' Speech (Who are you?), 8.
                h. Jonah's Statement and Response of Fear, 9-10*a*.
              g2. Sailors' Speech (What have you done?), 10*b*.
          f2. Narrative (Implications of Jonah's Flight), 10*c*.
        e2. Sailors' Speech (What shall we do to you?), 11.
      d2. Jonah's Command (Throw me into the sea!), 12.
    c2. Narrative (sailors try to row back to land), 13.
  b2. Sailor's Prayer (to Yahweh about Jonah's death), 14.
a2. Narrative (Jonah Ejected; Storm Stops) and Response of Fear, 15-16).

THE STORM BEGINS (4-5*a*).

As we begin this section, we encounter two key words involving the action of Yahweh and the responses of the sailors. Yahweh "sent a great wind"; the sailors "were afraid." The Hebrew word translated "sent" (*ṭûl* [797], though not commented on in TWOT) appears four times in the passage. Yahweh "threw" a great storm onto the sea; the sailors responded by "throwing" the cargo into the sea (1:5*b*). But this action has no effect, for it is only when they "threw" *Jonah* into the sea (1:12, 15) that the sea grew calm.

"Fear" (*yārē'* the verb [907] and *yir'â* the noun [907*b*]) is also crucial to the episode, framing the narrative. As the storm began, the sailors became "afraid." When Jonah announced that he "fears" Yahweh (1:9, NASB), this intensified the fear of the sailors (1:10; [907] and [907b]). But Jonah's confession is the turning point of the story—for the sailors. For when the storm subsided, their ignorant "fear" of the storm had heightened to reverent "fear" of Yahweh (1:16), on the same level as Jonah (2:9).

The words used also recall the creation account (Gen. 1:2, 9-10), where Yahweh controlled the sea by his Spirit, the same word as "storm" (*rûaḥ* [2131*a*]). In case we missed this, Jonah reminds us that Yahweh is "the God of heaven, who made the sea and the land" (1:9). "The sea" is found in these thirteen verses eleven times (1:4[2x], 5, 9, 11[2x], 12[2x], 13, 15[2x]) to emphasize its overpowering presence and continual threat to the existence of the boat, the sailors, and Jonah (cf. 2:4). But in the final analysis, it simply served Yahweh; He used it to His ends and no one was hurt.

None of these resolutions, however, are clear at the outset. The storm arose; the sea raged; the ship groaned under the strain; the veteran seamen trembled in terror.

THE SAILORS' FIRST PRAYER (5*b*)

The hardened, "godless" sailors realized their grave situation, and in desperation each cried out "to his own god." The sailors were most likely Phoenician, and would have pleaded with Baal or Melqart, their god of rain and thunder, who incidently was perceived as the master of Yamm, the god of the sea. Though now crying in ignorance (cf. 3:9) and in vain (cf. 2:8), they will eventually realize that Yahweh is the Creator of heaven and earth, and they will take His name in faith (1:14-16).

CARGO EJECTED; JONAH SLEEPS (5*c*-6*a*)

The sailors' short-lived piety did not pay off and they soon took matters into their own hands. They threw anything loose, including the cargo, into the sea "to lighten the ship." This would hopefully make the ship more manueverable, and thus give it a better chance against the storm (cf. Acts 27:18-19).

Meanwhile beneath the deck was a tired Jonah—yet another surprise! Exhausted from his flight, Jonah had fallen deeply asleep in the hold of the ship. How ironic that the only one who would understand what was happening, who could effectively pray and act, was dead to the world, while the sailors trembled in ignorance, prayed with no effect, and acted to no avail!

But Jonah was soon roused by the "captain," or first mate (Heb., "chief of the sailors"), who had no doubt gone "below deck"[5] to find more cargo to jettison. However, among the packages he discovered a prophet.

THE CAPTAIN'S COMMAND (6b)

The captain commanded Jonah to help find the solution to their problem, and later Jonah gave the command that does (1:12). Notice the splendid irony as this pagan sailor exhorts the prophet of Yahweh to pray! And again we see literary irony in the vocabulary, for the captain's command "Get up and call" is exactly the command Jonah is running away from ("Arise . . . and cry," 1:2 NASB)!

The exasperated rebuke was followed by a desperate plea. The captain and crew had all cried to their gods without success. Now that another individual had been discovered, perhaps *his* god would answer. The word "god" is properly in lower case, as it refers to the captain's theology (1:5), not Jonah's.

"Maybe he will take notice of us, and we will not perish" is parallel to the Ninevites' cry of 3:9. In both cases, their hopes and prayers *were* answered by the God of Jonah. Yahweh did "take notice," did "spare a thought" (NEB, JB), though Jonah in his callous indifference could not seem to care less.

---

5. Some point to this word (*s^eepînâ* [1537b], though not commented on in TWOT) as evidence of Aramaic influence on the book, and thus of a late date. But as many commentators point out, the word could easily be Phoenician in origin—as were the sailors (Allen, p. 187)—and therefore it cannot be used to establish the date.

THE SAILORS' FIRST SPEECH (7*a*)

Where we expect to hear a prayer or speech from Jonah in response to the captain's impassioned plea, we are surprised to hear the desperate voices of the crew. At least to this point Jonah was consistent; he was willing to let both Nineveh and the Gentile sailors perish in the ignorance of Yahweh.

The sailors' speech is simple, as are the three that follow, probing the situation to try to bring order from chaos. They proposed to "cast lots" to discover the individual responsible for the "calamity" ("evil," see comments on 1:2). This statement reveals several elements of their theology. They believed that they were trapped in some god's judgment against an individual among them. Further, they believed that this individual could be singled out to take his just deserts alone. Finally, they believed that the lot could determine the guilty party (as was possibly the case in Josh. 7:10-18).

THE LOT FALLS TO JONAH (7*b*)

The narrative finally does return to Jonah, but not by his choice. Though shooting in the dark, the sailors hit the target. The lot they cast was in the hand of Yahweh (Prov. 16:33) and pointed out Jonah as the man of the hour. He could no longer claim anonymity, hide in the hold, or maintain his silence.

THE SAILORS' SECOND SPEECH (8)

Seeing at last the possibility of finding some answers and saving their lives, the sailors pelted Jonah with five rapid-fire questions. The first echoes verse 7, "trouble" being the same Hebrew word as "calamity." Though Jonah did not answer this one directly at first (1:9), they deduced from his other answers that he was responsible before his actual confession in 1:12.

We also do not read of his answer to "What do you do?" But by 1:10*b* we can assume that he had told them his occupation while explaining why he was running away from Yahweh's service. The final three questions about his origins, his country, and his people could all provide answers about his religion, and thus about the god he had offended. These questions Jonah answered immediately.

JONAH'S REPLY AND THE SAILORS' RESPONSE (9-10*a*)

This verse-and-a-half is the center of the chapter, revealing Jonah as the source of the storm and bringing the sailors' fear to its highest point. With his first reply, "I am a Hebrew," Jonah answered the last three questions. The word "Hebrew" was the label by which an Israelite would have been known by non-Israelites (Gen. 40:15; Ex. 1:19). From this the sailors could deduce his religion, but Jonah presents that directly.

"I worship Yahweh" was not a pious answer; it identified Jonah's God, the one he revered or "fears" (see comments on 1:5). Rather than leave the sailors to their deductions, Jonah described Yahweh in such a way as to relate Him directly to their situation. Yahweh is "the God of heaven, who made the sea and the land." Yahweh is not a local, limited deity (cf. 1 Sam. 4:5-7; 1 Kings 20:28). He does not do battle with the elements, as do the gods of Phoenicia and Canaan; He made them, He is sovereign over them. Both the sea that threatened their existence and the land for which they longed are in the hand of Yahweh the Creator God.

The sailors responded with fear, as in 1:5 and 1:16. The Hebrew construction emphasizes the intensity of their response, "the men feared a great fear." Taking 1:5 into account, this communicates the peaking of their terror. But taking 1:16 into account as well (for it is verbally identical with the phrase in v. 10) we see the *meaning* of "fear" beginning to change.

Though Jonah had not wanted to "evangelize" the crew, his brief statements and actions did eventually result in their salvation. Jonah's fear ("worship") of Yahweh affected their fear of the storm and the sea. The sailors needed no longer tremble in ignorance, they now had a focus in Yahweh. And as they saw how He responded to their prayers and to Jonah's actions, their fear became Jonah's worship. This pattern was essentially repeated in Nineveh in chapter 3.

THE SAILORS' THIRD SPEECH (10*b*)

As we begin to work back through the symmetrical outline, this brief outburst parallels the series of questions in verse 8. "What have you done!" is not a question, but an exclamation, as the rest of the verse goes on to explain.

IMPLICATIONS OF JONAH'S FLIGHT (10*c*)

The sailors' outburst was prompted by their sudden realization of the implications of Jonah's earlier statements. "They knew he was running away from Yahweh, because he had already told them so"; so the crew exclaimed, "What have you done!" The order is reversed to show the immediacy of their response (and also to continue the chiastic structure). The writer similarly does not reveal *why* Jonah ran from Yahweh in 1:3, but waits to bring their conversation to light with greater impact in 4:2. Still, many scholars read this part of verse 10 as though it were a later, explanatory addition.[6]

When had Jonah told them? As John Walton points out, Jonah may have told the crew of his flight as he embarked the ship. (The language *is* identical to that of v. 3.) But only in light of his revelation of the universal and sovereign nature of his God do they put two and two together to realize that his flight created their plight.[7]

THE SAILORS' FOURTH SPEECH (11)

The *New International Version* has reversed the order of the two main clauses of verse 11 (cf. NASB). The verse begins

6. Julius A. Bewer, "A Commentary on Jonah," pp. 36-37.
7. Walton, p. 26.

with the sailors' final question, "What should we do to you to make the sea calm down for us?" This parallels their first speech, in which they proposed casting lots to discover the party responsible for the calamity (1:8). The rest of the verse can be translated as their own urgent description of the calamity, "the sea is getting rougher and rougher!"[8]

The episode is moving at a furious pace now. Following the rapid-fire questioning of verse 8, Jonah's confession of his identity in 9, and the terrified response of 10, the sailors demanded to know what they could do to Jonah to appease his God before the sea smashed their ship to pieces.

JONAH'S COMMAND (12)

In verse 6*b*, the captain had commanded Jonah to get up and pray, that he might have a hand in settling the storm and saving their lives. Jonah had gotten up, but had not prayed. We see later (4:3, 8) that Jonah would rather die than preach repentance to the Gentiles. But as he looked into the faces of each and every crewman whose lives were in his hands, he did not hesitate to act in compassion and at the expense (he believed) of his own life.

His startling command, "Pick me up and throw me into the sea" (see comments on 1:5*a*) was followed by two reasons. The first answered their immediate question: "Then the sea will become calm for you" (NASB). The second answered the sailors' first two probes as to "who is responsible for this calamity" (1:7, 8), formally confirming what they had already deduced. Thus, all that they had sought they found; every question was answered. Now they had only to act!

A FEEBLE ALTERNATIVE (13)

The narrative again takes us by surprise. We would have expected the exasperated mariners to have instantly grabbed the wayward prophet and tossed him overboard. But their response demonstrated a compassion for human life far

8. Allen, p. 206.

beyond Jonah's hardened indifference.

In exact parallel to verse 5, the crew members again tried to escape their dilemma by their own power. But though "the men did their best to row back to land," the God who made that land used His sea to keep them under His control. Certainly these old salts would have known their attempt would fail before they began. Yet they were willing to take the time, as "the sea grew even wilder than before" (identical in Hebrew to 1:11), and risk ship and soul to save the man responsible for their plight!

The compassion of the sailors was as instructive for Jonah (and his readers) as the repentance of Nineveh in chapter 3. The compassion toward their fellows and repentance toward Yahweh that was so sorely lacking in Jonah and his people came naturally to these ignorant heathen!

THE SAILORS' SECOND PRAYER (14)

The sailors' first prayer (1:5*a*) was both ignorant and ineffective, spawned by their fear of life-threatening forces they did not understand. But this second prayer came in light of knowledge and reverent fear. No longer did each cry "to his own god"; they all cried to Yahweh. They no longer prayed with their fingers crossed; they confessed His sovereignty over the situation: "you, O Yahweh, have done as you pleased" (cf. Dan. 4:35).

They were, however, still frightened. They did not want the responsibility for Jonah's death (as is clearly translated in the NIV). They did not want to "perish" for something they had not done (1:6); they did not now want to "die" (same Hebrew word, *'abad* [2]) for "taking this man's life . . . killing an innocent man." But since Yahweh had identified him as the one responsible for the storm, and since Jonah himself had not only confessed but had also clearly pointed out their course of action, they were ready to act in light of this revelation.

Why did Jonah ask the members of the crew to do what he could have done himself? Perhaps because he was answering their question (1:11*a*) directly. Perhaps he was simply afraid. But beyond this, whether Jonah intended it or not, their personal and physical involvement in this act of faith—for that is what it was—showed how their fear had changed from blind terror of the unknown to reverent fear of Yahweh.

THE STORM ENDS (15-16)

The situation was resolved as swiftly as it had arisen. The crew "picked up Jonah, [and] threw him into the sea" (NASB), in word-for-word fulfillment of his command (1:12). Without a break the narrative continues, "and the raging sea grew calm." "The sea," which had been a horrifying force in its ten previous occurences (see note on 1:4-5*a*), finally returned to normal in its last mention in the chapter.

And just as the sudden appearance of the storm had roused the men's fear (1:5*a*), its sudden disappearance again rouses their fear. But this time, "the men fear a great fear in relation to *Yahweh*" (Hebrew). The same phrase in verse 10 had had no stated object. As in verse 5, it had been blind terror. But in light of Jonah's confession, they observed the elements as in the hand of "Yahweh, the God of heaven, who made the sea and the land" (1:9). Their fear of Yahweh could then be translated "worship," as was Jonah's in verse 9.

Their actions confirm this. Sacrifice and vows were normal responses to Yahweh's saving grace (Ps. 50:14-15; 116:17-18) and were precisely Jonah's responses to his own salvation (2:9)! Yahweh in longsuffering had extended His salvation to the Gentiles despite every effort of Jonah to resist.

While the sailors profited greatly, physically and spiritually, from this encounter with Yahweh, Jonah was still on his downward spiral. We will pick up Jonah's story at the bottom of the sea in chapter 2.

JONAH AND JESUS

But first, it is impossible to resist making comparisons and contrasts between Jonah 1 and the gospel accounts of Jesus calming the storm (Matt. 8:23-27; Mark 4:36-41; Luke 8:22-25). Both episodes involved a man of God, a life-threatening storm, a boat full of terrified and helpless men, God's miraculous intervention mediated through the man of God, and the men's response of fear and wonder. Both men were asleep as the storm broke. Both were sought for help by the terrified mariners. Both brought about the end of the storm. Both inspired the fear of God by their actions and words.

Jesus, however, was walking with God, whereas Jonah was running from Him. Jonah's storm was a judgment on him that could have consumed the sailors as well; Jesus was in control of His storm and His disciples' well-being. Jesus intended His disciples to learn to act in knowledge and faith; Jonah did not care about the sailors. Jonah was revealed as a rebellious servant; Jesus as the Son of God. Jonah revealed Yahweh as Creator of the wind and the waves; Jesus was revealed as the Master of the wind and the waves—as Yahweh Himself.

2

YAHWEH SAVES JONAH

(JONAH 1:17—2:10)

Chapter 2[1] is the center of our symmetrical outline of Jonah. The prophet's salvation is sandwiched between the salvation of the sailors and Ninevites, as if to emphasize that the same Yahweh who is the Savior of Israel is also concerned to save the rest of the world: the Gentiles on the sea and the Gentiles on the land. After all, Jonah had confessed Him as the Sovereign of these realms (1:9)!

As with chapter 1, chapter 2 is well structured. The first and last statements involve Yahweh using a great fish to save Jonah from the angry sea and bring him safely to dry land. And in the midst of the narratives about the fish is a psalm composed by Jonah in the midst of the fish itself!

YAHWEH RESCUES JONAH FROM THE SEA (1:17)

"A GREAT FISH"

George Adam Smith has said, "This is the tragedy of the Book of Jonah, that a Book which is made the means of one of the most sublime revelations of truth in the Old Testament should be known to most only for its connection with a whale."[2] The "great fish" of 1:17 and 2:10 has given liberal critics reason to reject a historical interpretation of Jonah, has provided conservatives with a line of demarcation for

---

1. In the Hebrew Bible our 1:17 is 2:1. Thus all the verses of chapter 2 are one shy of the Hebrew numeration. The JB and the NJV, however, retain the Hebrew numeration.
2. George Adam Smith, "The Book of the Twelve Prophets," p. 679.

orthodoxy, and is the centering point of the allegorical pattern. The fish is, however, simply a humble servant of the saving God, prepared, commanded, and used, as were the storm and sea of chapter 1 and the vine, worm, and wind of chapter 4.

It is as foolish for the liberal to deny the possibility of taking the fish literally as for the conservative to attempt to identify the species of marine animal that could swallow and sustain a human being for three days and nights. Both slight the miraculous and the power of God. What Yahweh did to save Jonah is not normal; nor are the other divinely engineered encounters in the book. Storms at sea are commonplace, but not storms that rise and fall instantaneously. Plants sprout and grow, but not overnight. Worms eat and destroy vegetation, but not within a morning. Great fish devour people, but do not sustain them and disgorge them alive onto the shore.

The point of the "great fish" and all of the other agents by which Yahweh touches Jonah's life is that the Creator God is breaking into His ordered creation and literally moving heaven and earth to save His people. Each agent Yahweh specially prepares and "provides." The Hebrew word underlying "provided" in 1:17; 4:6, 7, and 8 (*mana* [1213]) demonstrates that these circumstances were not coincidences (cf. "assigned," Job 7:3; Dan. 1:5, 10; "appoint," Ps. 61:7). Yahweh worked with all levels of His creation—sea creatures, vegetation, creeping things, and the wind—to deal with His servant Jonah, and through Jonah with all of His chosen people.

Thus, what we know about the "great fish" is simply that it is a specially prepared and "provided" agent of Yahweh that saves Jonah from death at sea. The Hebrew word for fish (*dāg* [401a]) provides no insight for identifying the species involved. The creature could be any large fish or whale, or even something created for the moment.

Those of the allegorical school see the fish as symbolic of the monster Nebuchadnezzar/Babylon, who in Jeremiah

51:34 "swallowed" Israel into exile and in 51:34 is made to "spew out what he has swallowed," picturing the return from exile.[3] The major flaw of this interpretation, however, is that Jeremiah's swallowing is a judgment, whereas Jonah's is a salvation. The other details of the allegorical understanding fall apart under examination as well.[4]

"THREE DAYS AND THREE NIGHTS"

What of the "three days and three nights"? Many preachers and teachers, in view of Matthew 12:40, believe this time span is chosen specifically to create the type of Jesus' burial and resurrection. The allegorists see them as representative of the 70 years of captivity.

It might simply have taken the fish that long to return to shore. It could further emphasize Yahweh's amazing life-preserving activity, indicating a span of time far beyond that which any person could be expected to survive. "Three days" was also the length of time it took to journey through Nineveh (3:3), and quite possibly was the contemporary notion of the time it took to travel to the underworld.[5] This would fit well with the metaphors of the psalm, where Yahweh saves Jonah from "the depths of Sheol" (2:2) and brings him "up from the pit" (2:6).

Another strong possibility is that repentance and restoration was conceived as a three-day process, as by Jonah's contemporary, Hosea (6:1-2): "Come, let us return to Yahweh./. . ./After two days he will revive us;/on the third day he will restore us,/that we may live in his presence." This restoration to life "in his presence" is the opposite of Jonah's flight "away from Yahweh" (1:3, 10). Thus, besides indicating a length of time, the "three days" evokes the image of repentance, which is a major theme of the second half of the book.

3. Smith, pp. 687-88.
4. Gleason L. Archer, *A Survey of Old Testament Introduction,* pp. 308-9.
5. G. M. Landes, "The Kerygma of the Book of Jonah," pp. 11-12.

JONAH'S PRAISE OF YAHWEH'S SALVATION (2:1-9)

Verses 2 to 9 compose a Psalm of Declarative Praise (discussed below). Verse 1 serves as an introduction to the psalm, much like the titles or superscriptions of the Psalms from which Jonah draws (e.g., Ps. 18). Verse 10 parallels 1:17, framing the psalm that praises Yahweh's salvation with the narrative of that salvation.

INTRODUCTION (1)

Many scholars believe the psalm of praise is misplaced, and that a prayer for deliverance should follow this introduction. This is based on two misunderstandings. First, the word "prayed" (*pālal* [1776]) does not require an intercessory prayer to follow. In fact, the other use of this word in Jonah (4:2) also refers not to a petition, but to a conversation. Second, in "the belly of the fish" Jonah was saved from "the belly of Sheol" (JB). He did not pray for deliverance *from* the fish, but praised Yahweh for delivering him *by* the fish.

Notice the impact of a simple pronoun: "Jonah prayed to Yahweh *his* God" (cf. 1:5-6). Jonah was no longer running from the service of Yahweh, though his attitude was not yet totally redeemed. He had recovered the joy of his salvation, the bliss of right relation to "Yahweh *my* God" (2:6).

THE FORM OF THE PSALM (2:2-9)

This psalm follows the form of the Psalm of Declarative Praise (of the Individual), as identified and developed by Claus Westermann.[6] This kind of psalm is the response of one who has been saved to the salvation of Yahweh, and appears throughout the Scriptures. Its standard form fits Jonah well and provides an outline for analysis:

I. Proclamation ("I will praise You") (1?)
II. Introductory Summary (2)

6. Claus Westermann, *Praise and Lament in the Psalms,* pp. 102-16.

Is this psalm a verbatim reproduction of Jonah's prayer from the belly of the fish? Certainly, Jonah prayed more than these few lines during his 72-hour sojourn! But also as certainly, this psalm is a carefully constructed representation of the cumulative tone of the many prayers that Jonah offered to Yahweh during this time. The structured form and standardized hymnic vocabulary bear witness to a polished literary construction, rather than a spontaneous, emotional outburst.

The form of other psalms helps us understand Jonah 2, and so do their vocabulary and content. For the vocabulary of the psalm is quite different than the rest of the book. This reinforces the convictions of those who view the psalm as a later addition. However, there are also some very significant connections, as we will see.[7]

These critics also point out that almost every line has direct verbal parallels in the Psalter, thus arguing for its secondary nature. But chapter 2 is parallel to chapter 4, in which a key passage from the law (Ex. 34:6) is the basis of Jonah's language and actions. As the vocabulary of chapter 4 displays Jonah's grounding in the law of Yahweh, the vocabulary of chapter 2 shows his roots in traditional, faithful worship of Yahweh.[8]

Ironically, Jonah's response in chapter 2 is positive, for *he*

7. Cf. Leslie C. Allen, *The Books of Joel, Obadiah, Jonah and Micah*, p. 182n.
8. Brevard S. Childs, *Introduction to the Old Testament as Scripture*, pp. 423-24.

has been saved; in chapter 4 his response is negative, because *Nineveh* has been saved. Yet both were saved by the same Yahweh whose nature and actions were revealed by the Scriptures quoted!

INTRODUCTORY SUMMARY (2)

Most Psalms of Declarative Praise begin with a proclamation of praise, such as "I will praise Yahweh." Unless verse 1 functions as this proclamation ("Jonah prayed to Yahweh his God"), Jonah's psalm begins with the summary of what he is praising God about.

From the first line on, we are struck with the verbal parallels to the Psalter, especially the Psalms of David. Remarkably, the images of drowning that David often used as metaphors of his distress (e.g., Ps. 18) are *not* metaphorical in Jonah, they are literal!

We noticed parallelism of blocks of material in Jonah 1. In the Psalm we see parallelism of individual lines. Most modern versions (except the NASB and NKJV) lay out the text of such poetry with indentation to show this parallelism (noted here by the symbol //). Thus in verse 2:

In my distress // From the depths of the grave
I called to Yahweh, // I called for help,
and he answered me. // and you listened to my cry.

We learn from such parallels by noticing synonyms, antonyms, specifications, amplifications, and metaphors. Jonah's "distress" is specified as being in "the depths of the grave." The *Jerusalem Bible* notes the conceptual parallel of this new location to the location from which Jonah was saved (1:17; 2:1) by translating the former "the belly of the fish" and the latter "the belly of Sheol." Though the Hebrew words are different (*mē'eh* [1227a] in 1:17; 2:1 and *beṭen* [236a] in 2:2), they are often paralleled to denote inward parts of any sort (Ezek. 3:3), or the female womb in particular (Gen. 25:23; Isa. 49:1).

"The grave" (NIV) is the Hebrew word *she'ôl* (2303c). Also translated as "hell" (KJV, NKJV) or transliterated as "Sheol" (RSV, NEB, JB, NJV), *Today's English Version* best captures its meaning with "world of the dead."

Sheol is pictured in Scripture as beneath the ground (Job 17:16; Ezek. 31:15-17; Amos 9:2), a place of darkness (Job 10:19-22) and silence (Ps. 6:5; 31:17). All mankind goes there (Ps. 89:48), though the righteous hope to be redeemed whereas the wicked remain (Ps. 49:14-15). For though being in Sheol implies separation from God (Ps. 88:3-6), it is a place accessible to God (Ps. 139:8; Amos 9:2). Although it is the realm of the dead, some passages imply continued activity (Isa. 14:9-10), from which many derive a theology of the afterlife similar to that of other ancient peoples.[9]

Whether as simple in meaning as "the grave" where dead bodies are put, or whether it implies a realm of existence after death, Sheol is a place associated with death and not life. Jonah's point is that he was saved from certain death.

"I cried out and Yahweh answered" is a pattern so common to the Psalter that it needs no documentation. However, it is interesting to note those psalms that deal with deliverance from the sea (Ps. 18:4-6, 16-19; 69:13-18) and from Sheol (Ps. 86:1-4, 13). Interestingly, David in Psalm 86 also bases his salvation on Yahweh's attributes as revealed in Exodus 34:6 (see Appendix).

Notice in the final parallels the change from third to second person. This probably testifies that such psalms originated as genuine prayers, directed to Yahweh in the second person ("you"), and were later adapted to public worship, where the individual praises Yahweh before the community in the third person ("he"). Such change of person is common (Ps. 64; 66; etc.), as is the change from first person singular ("I") to plural ("we" [Pss. 75; 123; etc.]).

---

9. George A. Buttrick, ed., *Interpreter's Dictionary of the Bible*, s.v. "Dead, Abode of the."

LOOKING BACK TO THE TIME OF NEED (3-6*a*)

Following the introductory statement that praises Yahweh for His saving grace, this section details the distress from which Yahweh saved Jonah. Clearly, all of the imagery indicates that Jonah was saved from drowning.

"You hurled me into the deep." After the repetition of vocabulary for "throwing" in chapter 1 (see comments on 1:4-5*a*), we are surprised to find a different term here for "hurled" (*shālak* [2398]). The use of this word could indicate that Jonah's psalm was adapted from one that already existed, and that it retained its unique vocabulary.[10] The term is used elsewhere of God's casting someone "from His presence" in judgment (Ps. 51:11; 102:10) and His hurling Israel's "iniquities into the depths of the sea" (Mic. 7:19). Whether Jonah was quoting or creating, he retained the concept of "throwing," but used this term to underline the punitive nature of the throwing. Though the sailors physically tossed him into the sea, Yahweh was the one responsible for that act of judgment.

"The deep" (Ps. 68:22; 69:2; 88:6; 107:23) is parallel to "the heart of the seas" (Ps. 46:2; Ezek. 27:4, 25, 26, 27; 28:2, 8). Both are regularly seen as places of trauma, to which Yahweh sends the wicked in judgment and from which Yahweh saves the righteous. In Jonah, these locations are the literal loci of his distress, for which "Sheol" was metaphorical.

This picture is intensified by the next parallel couplet. "Currents" translates a word normally used of rivers (*nāhār* [1315a]), which has recently been discovered in literature contemporary to the Psalms with the meaning "sea" (Ps. 24:2; 89:25).[11] "Waves and breakers" (*mashbār* [2321d] and *gal* [353a]) appear together only in Psalm 42:7, in a line identical to Jonah's.

10. Landes, pp. 7-10.
11. Allen, p. 214.

Terrifying as this imagery is—especially to a Hebrew with little love for the ocean—Jonah startles us with his next words. His concern amid the crashing and churning currents was that he had "been banished from your [Yahweh's] sight" (v. 4)! But was not that what he had sought (1:3, 10)? In "the very heart of the seas" (v. 3) Jonah himself has a change of heart and recognizes his wrong in running from Yahweh when he experiences the full effects of his banishment. For in the Psalms this word is only used of Yahweh banishing the nations before His people (78:55; 80:8)!

"Yet I" (v. 4) is the turning point of the psalm, though many versions and commentators read the Hebrew word *'ak* (84) as *'êk*, "How?" (75b), continuing Jonah's lament of his situation (RSV, NEB, JB, LB, TEV, NJV).[12] It begins Jonah's confession of faith,[13] expressing his belief that Yahweh will act in accordance with His character and His commitment to His servant (2:6, 9). The hope of "yet I" is answered by the salvation of "But you" in verse 6.

"Your holy temple" is probably where the book of Jonah began[14] (see comments on 1:3), and where he now desired to return for his second chance at obedience. It also appears in verse 7, prompting many analysts to see 3-4 and 5-7 as parallel.[15]

The *New International*'s footnote to "The engulfing waters threatened me" (v. 5) offers the alternate rendering, "The engulfing waters were at my *throat*." This second rendering of the word *nepesh* (1395a) is well attested in ancient literature and occurs in other versions (NEB, JB, TEV; cf. Ps. 69:2; Isa. 5:14 ["appetite"]; Jer. 4:10).[16] The concrete image of water "at my *throat*" clearly conveys the meaning "threatened my *life*," the more normal translation of the word.

---

12. Julius A. Bewer, "A Commentary on Jonah," pp. 45, 48.
13. Westermann, p. 74.
14. But see Michael C. Griffiths, "Jonah," p. 983.
15. Allen, p. 213.
16. Ibid., p. 217n.

In verse 7 this same word is translated "life," though in verse 6 (and 4:3, 8) "life" (and "live") translates the synonym *ḥayyîm* (644f). This vocabulary connects the psalm to 1:14, and contrasts dramatically with 4:3, 8. Though the waters threaten Jonah's "throat"/"life" (2:5) to the point that his "life" is ebbing away (2:7), Yahweh saves him so that the sailors need not be charged with his "life" (1:14). By contrast, though Jonah praises Yahweh for saving his "life" from the pit, following the salvation of Nineveh he exclaims that "death would be better than life" (4:3, 8) and "he asks his life to die" (4:8, lit. Hebrew).

The responses of Jonah and the sailors to the threat to his "life" in chapters 1-2 emphasize their strongly positive feelings about human life. This makes the negative feelings Jonah has for his life in chapter 4 all the more amazing, and highlights his strongly negative feelings about the lives of the Ninevites.

The word for "the deep" in verse 5 (*tehôm* [2495a]) is different from that in verse 3, but is synonymous (Ex. 15:5; Job 41:31-32). "Seaweed was wrapped around my head" nicely parallels the rendering, "the engulfing waters were at my throat," making all three lines of the verse synonymous.[17]

In verse 6 Jonah's downward spiral as he runs from Yahweh ends when he sinks down "to the roots of the mountains" (see comments on 1:3). Though this phrase is unique in biblical literature, it does occur in the apocryphal book Ecclesiasticus (16:29), where it is parallel to "the foundations of the earth." Though unusual, the meaning of the image is clear: You don't get any lower than this!

Alongside this is another unique picture: "the earth

17. Many commentators (e.g., J. Vernon McGee, *Thru the Bible* [Nashville: Nelson, 1982], 3:752-53) see Jonah's death and resurrection in this psalm, and especially in this verse. Apparently it makes for a better type. However, identical language used by David in other Psalms (e.g., 16:10; 18:4-6), the suggested parallelism of "head" to "throat," and the dramatic contrast between Jonah's prayer for life and his prayer for death (4:3, 8) make this interpretation highly unlikely.

beneath barred me in forever." This very difficult Hebrew
phrase is, word-for-word, "the earth, her bars, around (or
behind) me forever." Most understand "the earth" as the
underworld,[18] especially in parallel to "the pit" (*shaḥat*
[2370d]; cf. Job 17:13-14; Ps. 16:10). Sheol is often pictured
as having a gate (Ps. 9:13; Isa. 38:10; Matt. 16:18); thus its
"bars" symbolize the locking up of Jonah in the land of the
dead: "I went down to the underworld,/Its bars closed behind me for ever."[19]

REPORT OF DELIVERANCE (6*b*-7)

Just when it seemed that all was lost, "but" points out the
dramatic change in direction ("you brought my life *up* from
the pit") and tone of the psalm. The usual order of the report
of deliverance is (A) I cried out; (B) He heard; (C) He saved.[20]
But here we have (A) He saved (v. 6*b*); and (B) I cried out (7);
but no "He heard" other than in the introduction (v. 2).

Yahweh Saved Jonah (6*b*). The image of Yahweh saving
His righteous servant from Sheol/the pit is common in the
Psalms (16:10; 18:4-6, 16-19; 30:1-3; etc.). But though the
language would have been well known to Jonah, the experience was without doubt unparalleled! The confession,
"Yahweh *my* God" again contrasts the God who can and
does save with the worthless "gods" of the nations (1:5; 2:8).

Jonah Cried Out (7). Jonah appears to have held out until
the very last minute to plead with Yahweh for his life. "When
my life was ebbing away" again recalls the vocabulary of the
Psalter (Ps. 77:3; 107:5; 142:3; 143:4), as does "I remembered you, Yahweh" in distress (Ps. 77:3, 11).

"Remembering" (*zākar* [551]) does not imply forgetting,
for God often "remembers" His people in their trouble. In a
most significant passage, Exodus 2:23-25, God "heard" the
groaning of Israel in bondage, He "remembered" His cove-

---

18. Bewer, p. 46.
19. Allen, p. 214.
20. Westermann, p. 103.

nant with Abraham, Isaac, and Jacob, He "looked" on the
Israelites and "was concerned" (intimately involved) with
them. In Exodus 3:7-8 Yahweh informs Moses that He had
"heard," had "looked," and was "concerned," but He was
no longer "remembering"; He had "come down" to deliver
His people from Egypt and into the land of promise.

Thus "remember" takes on the meaning, "to act on the
basis of commitment." In Exodus 2:25—3:8 it means Yahweh acted on the basis of His covenant with Abraham (Gen.
15:13-16) to deliver His people from Egypt and judge the
Egyptians for their harsh treatment. In Jonah, "remembering" Yahweh means calling upon His name as the God who is
there, mighty to save (cf. the name as revealed in Exodus
3:5-15).

Jonah's prayer "rose" to Yahweh, similar in concept
(though not terminology) to the wickedness of Nineveh that
"came up before" Him (1:2). The prayer rose "to your holy
temple" (cf. 2:4). Many commentators are certain this temple
is not the building in Jerusalem, but the heavenly palace of
Isaiah 6.[21] However, Jonah expected to "look again toward"
it (2:4). Further, eight times in Solomon's prayer of dedica-
tion (1 Kings 8:23-53; 2 Chron. 6:14-42) the extreme
significance of praying "toward the temple" is stressed.
Regardless of where God's people were, even in a land of captivity (for Jonah, Sheol), if they humbled themselves and
prayed toward the Temple in Jerusalem, Yahweh would
answer from heaven, His dwelling place (cf. Ps. 3:4).

PRAISE TO YAHWEH FOR HIS LOYAL LOVE AND SALVATION (8, 9*b*)

Jonah sandwiched his concrete response to Yahweh's saving acts, his vow to praise (9*a*), between two strong statements
of praise. The first powerfully contrasts the loyal love of
Yahweh to the utter worthlessness of idols; the second simply
and strongly states, "Salvation comes from Yahweh!"

21. Griffiths, p. 983.

54   *Jonah and Nahum*

The Hebrew of verse 8 is as difficult to translate as that of
6*a*. But most versions come up with a text roughly equivalent
to that of the *New International Version*. Psalm 31:6*a* is near-
ly identical to verse 8*a*. "Cling" (*shāmar* [2414]) usually con-
notes paying careful attention to or guarding something,
often God's law or ways (Ps. 18:21; 19:11). The form used in
Jonah appears only once and could mean to "carefully regard
(the name or deity of a god)."[22]

"Worthless idols" is rendered in the King James Version
"lying vanities." "Worthless" (*hebel* [463a]) is the key word
of Ecclesiastes (36 occurences). It serves here to emphasize the
value of the "idols," though it can mean "idol" by itself
(e.g., Deut. 32:21; 1 Kings 16:13, 26). "Idols" (*shāw'*
[2338a]) is a synonym for "worthless" (Zech. 10:2) and is
also used of false gods (Ps. 18:21; Jer. 18:15).

The reason these "idols" or false gods are worthless is that
they do not answer; they have no power to save; they offer no
loyal love (NIV "grace" [*ḥesed* (698a)]). Some versions and
commentators believe the second line means that those who
worship false gods have forsaken their loyalty to Yahweh
(RSV, TEV). Others think it means they have forsaken
Yahweh, "the Loyal One" (NKJV).[23] Most believe that the
false worshipers forfeit the "loyal love," "grace," or "mer-
cy" they could have from Yahweh (NIV, JB, LB).[24] This is
reinforced by Jonah's confession in 4:1, where he states that
Yahweh is "abounding in love (*ḥesed*)." (For more on this
term, see the Appendix.)

THE RENEWED VOW OF PRAISE (9*a*)

When faced with death, most people bargain with God,
promising Him anything to keep them alive. In the Psalms of
Lament, the "vow of praise" could be misunderstood that

22. G. R. Driver, quoted in Allen, p. 215.
23. John Walton, *Jonah*, p. 34; Bewer, p. 47.
24. Allen, p. 218.

way. "Set me free from my prison, that I may praise your name" (Ps. 142:7) could be seen as bargaining with God. However, because the praise of Yahweh ("hallelujah") is the most-commanded activity in Scripture,[25] vowing to praise could also be seen as the sincere desire of the afflicted individual to be allowed to continue to perform God's will.

The renewed vows of praise in Psalms of Declarative Praise prove this. For now, there is no need for bargaining! The worshiper desires to praise Yahweh and, under no external pressure, vows to do so forever (Ps. 18:49; 30:12; 118:28). Jonah's renewed vow of praise fits exactly the response of the sailors when Yahweh saved them from the storm (1:16). Both "feared Yahweh," both "made vows," and both "offered [promised] sacrifices."

The final line of the psalm, the second statement of praise, is the very center of the book. That "Salvation comes from Yahweh" is clear in relation to the Gentile mariners of chapter 1, the Gentile Ninevites of chapter 3, and the Hebrew prophet of chapter 2. The book ends with Yahweh extending His salvation once again to Jonah in chapter 4. For though He obeyed Yahweh outwardly in going to Nineveh and preaching, he was still running away inwardly as the narrative closes.

YAHWEH RETURNS JONAH TO THE LAND (10)

The two simple lines of narrative that surround the psalm (1:17; 2:10) contrast markedly with the narrative concerning Jonah. Yahweh literally moved heaven and earth to get His prophet from 1:1 to 3:1, where he was willing to go to Nineveh. On the other hand, He had but to "provide" the fish to rescue Jonah from the sea and "command" the fish to return him to the dry land. If only God's people (including us!) were as obedient as the rest of His creation.

25. Westermann, p. 15.

3

YAHWEH SAVES NINEVEH

(JONAH 3:1-10)

The text of chapter 3 begins identically to chapter 1, and the contents parallel significantly:

Chapter 1	Chapter 3
I. Jonah is sent to Nineveh, 1-3	I. Jonah is sent to Nineveh, 1-3
II. Gentile sailors are threatened with destruction, 4-13	II. Gentile Ninevites are threatened with destruction, 4-7
III. Sailors cry to Yahweh, 14	III. Ninevites cry to God, 8-9
IV. Yahweh saves them from the storm, 15	IV. God saves them by relenting from threatened destruction, 10

JONAH GOES TO NINEVEH (1-4)

GOD CALLS—AGAIN (1)

Prophets do not always get a second chance. The disobedient prophet of 1 Kings 13 was mauled to death by a lion; after Elijah fled from Jezebel, Yahweh had him anoint Elisha as his successor (1 Kings 19:16). But chapter 3 begins just as chapter 1, sounding as though nothing had happened, but with one difference: "son of Amittai" has been replaced by "a second time." Yahweh had preserved Jonah's life to preserve the lives of Nineveh.

THE SECOND COMMISSION (2)

The second commission varies from the first (1:2) following the word "proclaim." The "wickedness" of the city is not mentioned. Perhaps it was mentioned initially to incite Jonah (and his readers) against the city, motivating him to proclaim its certain doom. Unlike his readers, however, Jonah knew that Yahweh was extending to Nineveh the opportunity to repent and be saved (4:2). But now, after being forgiven by Yahweh for his own wicked rebellion, Jonah was willing to go—though more out of chastening than because of compassion. Jonah (and his readers) would now understand that regardless of the reason, when Yahweh says "Go!" you simply respond, "Where?"

JONAH OBEYS (3)

The first line of verse 3 is exactly what we had expected to read in 1:3. Yahweh said, "Arise, go to Nineveh," "So Jonah arose and went to Nineveh" (NASB). Obedience is usually stressed in the Old Testament by using the same verbs in the fulfillment that were used in the command (e.g., 1 Kings 18:1-2). Here the obedience is doubly stressed with the phrase "according to the word of the LORD" (NASB; cf. Jer. 13:1-2).

The text is silent about Jonah's thoughts during the month or so it would have taken to travel the 500-600 miles to Nineveh (assuming the fish dropped him off somewhere around Joppa). But no doubt he thought a great deal about the "great city" (1:2, 3:2).

The rest of verse 3 amplifies on the greatness of Nineveh in a way that has generated a great deal of opinion. Nineveh had been founded by Nimrod after he had established the first Babylonian empire (Gen. 10:8-12), and archaeologists have found occupation of the site as early as 4500 B.C. The Nineveh Jonah would have known was extensively rebuilt by the Assyrian king Shalmaneser I (c. 1260 B.C.) and had been made an alternate royal residence to Asshur and Calah by Tiglath-pileser I (1114-1076 B.C.).

But because Nineveh was larger and more important after Jonah's time, as the major city and last capital of Assyria, and because its fall was synonymous with the fall of Assyria (as in Nahum), many scholars feel the composition of Jonah must date from after its fall in 612 B.C. But one could also argue that Nineveh was selected to receive the grace of Yahweh in Jonah's day to contrast with the judgment of Yahweh it would taste in Nahum's day. In that way it would remain an amazing example of more than a century of Yahweh's patience and longsuffering. This is certainly the *intention*, at least, of the author of Jonah.

Further, all writers who date Jonah after the exile read "Now Nineveh *was*" as a clear indication that the writer was citing an ancient memory. They argue further that the incredible size of Nineveh, "three days" around or across, is typical of such legendary exaggeration, for the Nineveh of Jonah's day was about three miles in circumference.[1] However, the construction of "Now Nineveh was" is the standard form of inserting a parenthetical statement into Hebrew narrative (cf. Gen. 13:2, NASB). All narratives are written in the past tense, and this construction cannot be construed as pointing to an ancient time. It cannot be used to prove the early or late date.

The same is true of the "three days' journey" (KJV). Most versions leave the interpretation of that statement to the reader, though the *New International Version, Today's English Version,* and *Living Bible* offer explanations. Many conservative interpreters read (with the NIV and TEV), "it took three days to go all through it." As opposed to reading "three days' journey" as an absolute statement that Nineveh was 55 miles across or around,[2] we read a functional descrip-

---

1. Julius A. Bewer, "A Commentary on Jonah," pp. 50-51.
2. Leslie C. Allen, *The Books of Joel, Obadiah, Jonah and Micah,* p. 221.

tion of how much time it would take Jonah to work through the city.[3]

Another option is that this journey deals not only with Nineveh proper, but with its whole "administrative district."[4] This might gain support from Genesis 10:11-12, where Nineveh, Rehoboth-Ir, Calah, and Resen together seem to be labeled "the great city."

However understood, Nineveh was truly "a very large city," or "a city important to God" (NIV footnote). Most versions read *'ĕlōhîm* (93c) as an adjective (cf. Gen. 23:6; 30:8), rather than as the proper name "God." But God three times referred to Nineveh as the "great city" (1:2; 3:2; 4:11). The men of Sodom are referred to as "wicked and great sinners before Yahweh" (Gen. 13:13, lit. Hebrew) in a parallel construction, except that "Yahweh" cannot be so easily used as an adjective. In light of these considerations, the alternate rendering, "a city important to God," might be the best.[5]

JONAH PREACHES (4)

The message Yahweh had for Nineveh apparently contained, or was summed up, in only five (Hebrew) words: "Forty more days and Nineveh will be destroyed." "Destroyed" or "overthrown" (*hāpak* [512]) conjures up memories of the utter eradication of Sodom and Gomorrah, also destroyed for their wickedness (Gen. 19:25, 29; Deut. 29:23).

Why forty days? The number forty is often associated with judgment and/or testing, as in the rainfall of the Flood (Gen. 7:4, 12, 17), the days Israel spied out the land, as well as the years she spent in the wilderness (Num. 14:34), and the days Jesus spent in the wilderness (Matt. 4:2; Mark 1:13; Luke

3. John Walton, *Jonah*, p. 39.
4. J. D. Douglas, ed., *New Bible Dictionary,* s.v. "Nineveh."
5. Cf. Allen, p. 221.

4:2). Elijah, too, spent forty days and nights in the desert, being instructed by Yahweh in words and deeds after what he considered a failed mission (1 Kings 19). And in a fascinating parallel, Moses was on Sinai with Yahweh for forty days and nights, praying that Yahweh would not destroy Israel for the incident with the golden calf (Ex. 34:28; Deut. 9:18, 25)—the very setting in which the forgiving attributes of God quoted in 4:2 were originally given.

In another major surprise, Nineveh responded immediately and completely. The immediacy is stressed in Jonah's preaching for only one day, one-third of the potential mission. The completeness is developed in verses 5-9.

THE NINEVITES REPENT (5-9)

This section can be divided into three movements: The people repent (5); the king repents (6); and repentance proclaimed (7-9). Each section contains the word "sackcloth."

The People Repent (5). "The Ninevites believed God" is doubly surprising: first, because of the fact, second, because of the vocabulary. Critics of the historicity of Jonah consider this repentance to be the most amazing statement in the book.[6] But John Walton spends a great deal of time in his small commentary documenting the religious beliefs of the Assyrians relative to interpretation of omens and portents, whether given in the skies, by means of animals, or by diviners, Assyrian or foreign; and as Alcorn concludes,

> The severe plagues of 765 and 759 and the total eclipse of 763 B.C. could have been used by God to alert the people to their need; and certainly when combined with the work of the Spirit of God before and through His prophet there is sufficient cause for the great repentance recorded.[7]

The vocabulary, too, is amazing, for it is identical to the response of Abram in Genesis 15:6, the classic text on

6. Bewer, pp. 3-4.
7. Walton, pp. 40-48; Wallace A. Alcorn, "Jonah, Book of," p. 947.

justification by faith (Rom. 4:1-3). The only difference is that "Abram believed *Yahweh*," whereas "the Ninevites believed *God*." But this use of "God" parallels chapter 1, up to the point that the sailors came to know and fear Jonah's God, Yahweh. The Ninevites, however, never heard that name, but still responded to "the God" (Hebrew), that is, "this prophet's God," and were saved from, at least, the destruction.

I say "at least" because most commentators stress the limited insight and response of both the sailors and the Ninevites.[8] However, the parallel responses of the sailors and of Jonah to Yahweh ("fear," 1:16*a*//1:9 and "sacrifice and vows" 1:16*b*//2:9) and the parallel responses of the Ninevites and of Abram (above) imply to me a parallel faith; and thus a parallel response by Yahweh, counting it to them as righteousness.

Further, not only did they believe, they *acted*. "They declared a fast, and all of them, from the greatest to the least, put on sackcloth." It is not just that these are "Gentiles, who do not have the law, [but] do by nature things required by the law" (Rom. 2:14); these were common acts of repentance in the ancient world. But they also form a stunning parallel to the response Joel demands of Israel (1:8, 13-14; 2:12), especially in light of the verbal agreement of Joel 2:14 to verse 9, and 2:13 to 4:2).

The King Repents (6). All Nineveh repented, the least and now the greatest. The phrase "king of Nineveh" is yet another in our series of difficulties noticed by critical interpreters. In Jonah's time, Nineveh was not yet the capital of Assyria; thus its ruler would not live in Nineveh, nor be called "king" of a city anyway. However, as noted above, Nineveh was indeed a royal residence at that time, and describing the king of a country as the king of a city is seen elsewhere in the Old Testament (1 Kings 21:1; 2 Kings 1:3) and also in Neo-Assyrian inscriptions.[9]

---

8. E.g., Walton, p. 44.
9. G. M. Landes, "Jonah, Book of," 5:490.

Perhaps a better solution is to be found in the meaning of the Hebrew word *melek* (1199a), for this word is much broader in meaning than simply "king of a country." And its Akkadian cognate, *malku*, is not normally used of the "king of a country," and could allow the translation "mayor of Nineveh," or "governor of the region of Nineveh."[10]

"The king" follows the lead of his people. He exchanges his "royal robe" for sackcloth, symbolizing acceptance of the affliction of God, and exchanges "his throne" for a seat in "the ashes" (NASB), symbolizing his prostration and utter humiliation before God. The "king" has been singled out from the people, just as the captain had been singled out from the crew in 1:6. Their statements have tremendous parallels, as seen in the following verses.

Repentance Proclaimed (7-9). All Nineveh, "from the greatest to the least" (v. 5), had begun their acts of repentance. Now all of their officials, "the king and his nobles," followed suit and proclaimed repentance as the law of the land. Not only were fasting and sackcloth required of the people, they were required of the animals as well. Though this amazing ritual has not (yet) been discovered in Assyrian literature, it is known from Persia. But again, this should not be used as a basis for dating.[11]

Rather, the repentance of the animals has a meaning within the book of Jonah and with reference to the book of Joel. When Yahweh sums it all up in 4:11, He explains that the concern Jonah has felt for a plant, He has felt for the higher order of His creation—not only the people, but the animals as well! And by parallel in Joel, the animals' suffering (as a result of the locust plague) is as valid a concern as the people's (1:18-20; 2:22).

The sincerity of their repentance is to be displayed in a series of acts: fasting, wearing sackcloth, urgent ("strong")

10. Walton, pp. 67-69.
11. Landes, 5:490.

praying to God, and giving up "evil ways" and "violence." "Violence" is exceptional cruelty to other human beings, a great guilt of the nations (Hab. 1:9; 2:8, 17) and also of Israel (Hab. 1:2, 3; Mic. 6:12). But the more general "evil ways" begins an extended word play over the next three verses.

This "evil" or "wickedness" (*rā'â* [2191c]) was the reason Jonah was first sent to preach against Nineveh (1:2). The Ninevites perceived this and repented. But they were not hoping that Yahweh would "repent" of *His* "evil" (*rā'âh* translated "destruction," v. 10, cf. 1:7, 8; 4:2) so they would not be destroyed. Then, when Yahweh does "repent of the evil," (KJV) this becomes "evil" ("greatly displeased") to Jonah (4:1)!

The first statement of verse 9 is verbally identical with Joel 2:14*a*, excepting the use of "God" again. God's relenting and turning is based on His forgiving attributes (Ex. 34:6) in both Joel (2:13) and Jonah (4:2). This impassioned plea, this crying out to the unknown God in hope of His compassion, and especially this desired end, "so that we will not perish," parallels directly the captain's plea in 1:6. And as Yahweh heard and responded to the sailors, so He hears and responds to the Ninevites.

YAHWEH RELENTS FROM HIS WRATH (10)

"Relent" or "compassion" (NASB, NKJV, NIV), is often rendered "repent" (KJV, RSV, and NEB). No doubt these former versions translate the words differently to avoid the question, "But how can God repent?" The word "repent" (*nāḥam* [1344]) has the range of meaning "to be sorry," "to comfort or be comforted" (as in "Nahum"), and "to change one's mind." It does not demand that the change of mind or acting is from doing evil to doing good, or that the one who changes his mind is fickle.

When Yahweh "repents" or "changes His mind" about a particular act of judgment, He is not changing His mind about His ultimate end. For example, Yahweh desired His people to worship Him only (Ex. 20:1-3) and pronounced judgment on them for making the golden calf (32:9-10). But when He "repented" at Moses' intercession (32:12, 14), it was not because He had been calmed down. He destroyed only the wicked among them, and retained the rest as a people wholly devoted to His name. He met His ultimate end of purging the idolatry from the people (cf. Ex. 20:3; 34:6-7).

Similarly in Jonah, Yahweh had announced judgment on Nineveh because of "its wickedness" (1:2). When the Ninevites turned from their evil, Yahweh turned from His wrath (3:10). The *New International Version* stresses the "compassion" of that response, the other versions the "change of mind." Regardless, His ultimate end is accomplished, because the "evil" is purged from Nineveh. But He did not have to bring upon them His "evil" in exchange for their "evil," but His "repentance" because of their "repentance."

Most commentators note the striking parallel between verses 8-10 and Jeremiah 18:7-8:

> "If at any time I announce that a nation or kingdom is to be uprooted, torn down and destroyed, and if that nation I warned repents of its evil, then I will relent and not inflict on it the disaster I had planned."

Again, those who date Jonah after the exile cite this use of Jeremiah as yet another piece of evidence. However, that Jeremiah simply states this principle as a decree of Yahweh, whereas Jonah carefully and persuasively develops the concept as though it was new (at least in relation to the nations) might indicate that Jeremiah *follows* rather than precedes Jonah.

Regardless, both clearly teach the principle that Yahweh will change His declared actions toward a nation based on that nation's change of heart and action (positively *or* negatively, Jer. 18:9-10). However, this monumental act of divine compassion causes poor Jonah no end of grief!

4

JONAH'S DISOBEDIENCE EXPLAINED AND CHALLENGED

(JONAH 4:1-11)

The narrative changes focus, from God's dealing with Nineveh to Yahweh's dealing with Jonah. But though the focus has changed, the nature of God's dealing is identical—He needs to save Jonah.

JONAH EXPLAINS HIS DISOBEDIENCE (1-3)

The terminology of 4:1-2 is identical to that of 3:9-10. To point this out, verse 1 could be translated, "But this was evil to Jonah with a great evil and it made him fiercely angry." As mentioned earlier (comments on 1:2), God turning from His "evil" ("destruction") because Nineveh had turned from its "evil" was "evil" to Jonah. Further, as soon as God had abandoned His fierce anger (*ḥārôn* [736a]), Jonah found it (*ḥārâ* [736]; 4:1, 4, 9 [twice]).

The narration lets us in on this word play, but Jonah was probably angered over Nineveh's repentance, which he could see, rather than over God's choice to relent, which he could not see. The forty days were not yet over (which is why he waited éast of the city to see what would happen, 4:5), but he knew now that Yahweh could indeed spare the Ninevites because of their response.

His complaint to Yahweh contains several remarkable and startling elements. First, his complaint is called a "prayer," the same word used in 2:1. But in chapter 2, Jonah praised Yahweh for saving him and giving him life. In chapter 4,

Jonah criticizes Yahweh for saving Nineveh and asks Him to take his life!

The second surprise is that the complaint explains Jonah's original disobedience. While "still at home," in Israel, Jonah spoke, and perhaps even warned Yahweh of the potential of Nineveh's response. It seems he was "so quick to flee to Tarshish" in order to save Yahweh the unthinkable necessity of saving the Ninevites should they repent!

Jonah based his logic on the "thirteen attributes" of God found in Exodus 34:6-7.[1] Following the heinous sin of idolatry with the golden calf, Yahweh Himself pronounced these characteristics, which marked him as the God who forgives (see Appendix). Jonah quotes only verse 6, just as Joel had quoted it to an Israel in need of repentance (Joel 2:13). But he adds, with Joel, the statement that these attributes imply that Yahweh "relents from sending calamity." This phrase is also taken, word-for-word, from the same context (Ex. 32:14).

Jonah gladly accepted Yahweh's forgiveness for Israel and for himself. In his poem (2:2-9) he had stated that his salvation had come from Yahweh's "grace," the same word as the abundant "love" of Yahweh here (*hesed* [698a]). However, Jonah would not have this forgiveness extended to the Gentiles, to Nineveh, (though this door had been opened in Ps. 145:8; see Appendix).

Our next surprise results from the remarkable contrast to Jonah's request in chapter 2. Three times (2:5, 6, 7), Jonah had praised Yahweh for saving his life. Now we read the first of two requests by Jonah that his life be taken (4:8)! Jonah's words, "take away my life," echo those of Elijah in 1 Kings 19:4, though Jonah sighs, "my death is better than my life" (Heb.) for Elijah's "I am no better than my ancestors." Both prophets felt that they had been defeated and that they had let Yahweh down. Elijah felt certain that he had broken the back

1. J. H. Hertz, *The Pentateuch and Haftorahs*, p. 970.

of Baalism on Mt. Carmel, and that he had handed Yahweh the victory (1 Kings 18). But Jezebel's fury sent him running 100 miles for his life. Convinced he was the only believer in Israel, he was ready to die in shame. But Yahweh, by words and by His creation, showed Elijah the divine perspective during his forty days and nights in the desert (1 Kings 19:5-18).

Jonah would now face an identical situation. Certain his mission of announcing judgment on Nineveh had failed, he was ready to die. But Jonah had forgotten Yahweh's perspective. Jonah's short-sighted self-centeredness is emphasized in the Hebrew by the use of the first person ("I, me, my") nine times (see NASB). As with Elijah, Yahweh would once again move heaven and earth to instruct His prophet—and thus all of His people, including us!

Yahweh Challenges Jonah's Anger (4)

Yahweh began to challenge and correct Jonah's perspective by using his own words. Jonah had evaluated his death as "good" ("better," *ṭôb* [793a]); Yahweh responded, literally "Is your anger also good?" (*yāṭab* [863], a related word). Both of Jonah's feelings are obviously wrong. The point is not "Have you any right to be angry?" but "Is your anger right?"

This same challenge appears in 4:9 and suggests the following scheme for the chapter:

- a1. Jonah explains his disobedience and his anger over Yahweh's saving Nineveh, 1-3
  - b1. Yahweh challenges Jonah's anger over His saving Nineveh, 4
    - c. God demonstrates salvation and destruction to Jonah, 5-8
  - b2. God challenges Jonah's anger over His destroying the plant, 9
- a2. Yahweh explains His saving of Nineveh, 10-11

The word "provide" and the change of the name of God
from "Yahweh" to "God" play key roles in this analysis.

GOD DEMONSTRATES SALVATION AND DESTRUCTION TO JONAH
(5-8)

Many interpreters, ancient and modern, have proposed
that the events of verse 5 took place before verse 1.[2] They
assume that Jonah burst out in anger at the end of the forty
days when nothing had happened to Nineveh. But that cannot
explain why he would decide to stick around for further examination.

G. M. Landes suggests that Jonah misunderstood Yahweh's question about his anger, taking it to mean that he
should not *yet* be angry, rather than that his anger was wrong
in itself. The implication is that Jonah's prophecy of destruction may yet be fulfilled.[3]

Jonah went "east of the city" because he had originally approached it from the west. His one-day journey through the
city must have been eastward, and after seeing the mass
repentance of the Ninevites, he just kept going eastward. The
"shelter" Jonah built was most likely constructed of
whatever branches and leaves were handy. The same word is
used of the temporary shelters ("booths") in which the
Israelites lived in the wilderness while they were being instructed by Yahweh (*sūkkâ* [1492d]; Lev. 23:42-43).

Jonah's thoughts were obviously not on his own state of
being. Like so many who hear a sermon (including Jonah's
readers), he apparently did not feel Yahweh's question dealt
with him. His concentration was on "the city," used three
times in this verse (Heb.). But Jonah's attention and actions
were both misdirected.

Jonah's shelter must have been a feeble structure, for he
was in "discomfort." Not until "Yahweh God provided a
vine" was he able to enjoy adequate shade. Simply as this

2. Leslie C. Allen, *The Books of Joel, Obadiah, Jonah and Micah*, p. 231n.
3. G. M. Landes, "The Kerygma of the Book of Job," p. 27.

verse reads, several terms make key connections with the narrative.

First, this plant was "provided," the same act of God that had brought the fish into Jonah's life to save him from drowning (1:17). Most versions (other than the LB) translate this word consistently here and in verses 7 and 8 to make its repetition apparent. And just as the fish had saved Jonah, the vine "saves" (Heb.) him from his "discomfort."

The word the *New International Version* renders "ease" is often used significantly of God's salvation (Ex. 3:8; 18:4, 8, 9, 10), in fact, three times in Psalm 18 (Title, 17, 48), which so regularly paralleled Jonah's own psalm. And what was Jonah saved from? His "evil"—once again, our key word (*rā'â* [2191c]) of 3:8—4:1. In a fascinating continuation of the word play, Yahweh God saved Jonah from his "evil" situation (being overheated), though not from his "evil" attitude (his fierce anger, v. 9).

Further significant terminology involves the One who provided: "Yahweh God." We saw above (comments on 3:5) that the name "Yahweh" had been consistently used of God's dealing with Jonah, whereas "God" had dealt with the Gentiles. But now both names are used to mark the transition to "God" dealing with Jonah. One implication of this is that God is now going to deal with Jonah the way Jonah would have Him deal with the nations. Further, it was "Yahweh God" who created Adam, thus all humanity, from the dust (Gen. 2:7) and placed him in the Garden of Eden (2:15), not far from where Jonah was sitting!

Jonah's response to Yahweh God's salvation is grammatically synonymous but emotionally antonymous to verse 1. Because God saved Jonah from the "evil" of discomfort, "Jonah rejoiced with a great joy" (Heb.); but because God saved Nineveh from the "evil" of destruction, "This was evil to Jonah with a great evil" (Heb.)!

One final comment about the "vine." Most commentators classify this plant as the fast-growing *Ricinus communis*

(NJV), the "castor oil plant" (JB). But as in the case of the "great fish," its identification and rate of growth are not as important as its function as the obedient servant of the saving God (see comments on 1:17).

Yahweh God had provided the vine as an agent of salvation. But as the sun prepared to rise the next day, "God provided" an agent of destruction: "a worm," a creeping thing.[4] The creature "attacked" (NASB) the sheltering vine, and it immediately drooped and "withered." Jonah was now without God's provision for salvation.

The sun rose, and to compound its searing presence, "God provided a scorching east wind." Earlier, Yahweh "threw" a wind onto the sea, which threatened the lives of Jonah and the sailors (1:4). Now God "provided" a wind in the desert that threatens Jonah's life on land. Denis Baly describes the brutal effects of this sirocco wind:

> While it is blowing, the temperature rises steeply, 16 to 22° F. (9-12° C.) above average. . . . Relative humidity drops by as much as 40 percent, and every scrap of moisture seems to have been extracted from the air. It is this intense dryness and the fine dust in the air which are so exhausting, for other hot days, though troublesome, do not have the same effect.[5]

Elijah, too, had been taught by God's great wind (1 Kings 19:11). Again, there is a possible connection of "wind" and "Spirit" here (see comments on 1:4-5a). Jonah, who had resisted the call of God's Spirit, was now in danger of his life by God's Spirit.

While the wind scorched, the sun "blazed on" Jonah's head. This word, which had described the worm's assault ("chewed") on the plant (*nākâ* [1364]), is also used of God's

---

4. Or "weevil," Allen, p. 233.
5. Denis Baly, *The Geography of the Bible* (New York: Harper & Row, 1974), p. 52.

acts of judgment against His disobedient people (Deut. 28:22 27, 28, 35).

As a result of the onslaught of the elements, Jonah "grew faint" (cf. Amos 8:13). Again quoting Elijah (1 Kings 19:4), "he asked his life to die" (Heb.). In 4:3 he had asked Yahweh to take his life, but now, experiencing God's destruction, he turned inward with his request. How opposite were the Ninevites, who did not even know God by name.

GOD CHALLENGES JONAH'S ANGER (9)

Once again, in response to Jonah's evaluation of his "good" ("better") death, God asks, "Is your anger also good concerning the vine?" (Heb., see comments on 4:4). This time Jonah understands the question clearly and snaps, "My anger is good—good enough to die about!" (Heb.). Jonah had been angry enough about Nineveh's repentance to desire death, even though he and they had tasted God's compassionate turning from destruction. But now, having tasted God's destruction, though Nineveh still stood, Jonah was convinced that death was his only good choice—a good enough choice to snap back at God about.

YAHWEH EXPLAINS HIS SAVING OF NINEVEH (10-11)

God could have continued to deal with Jonah as with a Gentile with whom He had no relation. He could have snapped back, "You jerk! Can't you get it through your thick skull that people are more important than plants!" But God once again dealt with Jonah as Yahweh, his Savior and Covenant God. He spoke softly to restore the prophet—and win over his readers (cf. 1 Kings 19:12-18; Hosea 2:14).

Yahweh's gentle answer contrasts the shallow, self-serving concern Jonah had for his shade plant with the deep, well-founded concern Yahweh has for His own creations, not just those made in his image, but the animals and plants as well.

The word "concern" (*ḥûs* [626]) also carries the connotation of "pity" (KJV, RSV, NEB) with the result of sparing from harm or withholding judgment. The word appears five times in the book of Deuteronomy, where Yahweh commands his people *not* to "pity" and "spare" those who deserve death, Jew (13:9; 19:13, 21; 25:12) or Gentile (7:16).

The word is also used in Ezekiel of Yahweh not pitying or sparing His own people from judgment (Ezek. 5:11; 7:4, 9; 8:18; 9:5, 10). But it also speaks of His pitying and sparing Israel in her infancy (16:5-14; 20:17), her ignorance. Only when Israel had truly earned her judgment by throwing Yahweh's law back in His face did He turn from pity without hope of relenting (24:14).

Jonah was "concerned" about the vine because it "saved" him from his "evil" situation. It gave him great joy. Yet he had no part in planting, nourishing, or growing the vine. Further, "It sprang up overnight and died overnight." They had no history together, Jonah had no investment in the vine.

Yahweh, on the other hand, is the Creator of all mankind. He did plant. He did tend. He did cause growth. So He immediately contrasts His concern in verse 11. "How about *me*? Should I not be concerned about Nineveh, that great city?" (Heb. order, reversed in NIV). After all, Israel can pray for Yahweh's concern when they repent ("spare," Joel 2:17). Yahweh details the "greatness" of the city to contrast further with the insignificance of the plant.

The "hundred and twenty thousand people who cannot tell their right hand from their left" are often considered children (TEV; cf. Isa. 7:16; 8:4).[6] But in context, the whole of Nineveh is in view, all who repented, both people *and* animals (3:8). This also is an excellent estimate of the population of Nineveh in Jonah's day.[7] The idiom does not assume absolute innocence, but ignorance of Yahweh (3:9; 1:5). And as

6. Julius A. Bewer, "A Commentary on Job," p. 63.
7. J. D. Douglas, ed., *New Bible Dictionary,* s.v. "Nineveh."

Yahweh had spared the sailors in their ignorance, so he spared Nineveh.

The last Hebrew phrase in the book, "and many cattle as well," sounds odd at first. But Yahweh is contrasting Jonah's concern for a plant to His own concern for the higher orders of creation, people and animals. The animals, like the people, had repented. Yahweh acts in loyal love to His people (2:8; 4:2) and to his creatures (Ps. 136:25; Matt. 6:26).

EPILOGUE

The book of Jonah ends with a question. The obvious answer is "Yes!" Yes, Yahweh should show concern for all of His creation, especially those who do not realize their wrong and their need for repentance.

We do not hear Jonah's response. Let us hope that he was trapped by divine logic and taken by divine love. But what of his readers? Their empathy with Jonah must have been strong. They had fled with Him, though perhaps as much in fear as in hatred of brutal Nineveh. They had hidden with him in the hold, prepared to die by God's hands rather than by Assyrian atrocities.

But perhaps they had also seen the frightened faces of the sailors who looked to Jonah as their only hope of life. Perhaps they applauded his self-sacrifice for the survival of the innocent crew. Certainly they were startled at the Gentiles' response to Yahweh.

They would have reveled with Jonah in the God of the Psalms, who saves His righteous servants like no worthless idol can. Chastened, they would have entered Nineveh with bold proclamations of doom. But how would they have responded when the Ninevites instinctively repented after the pattern of Joel?

They would have run to the desert, like Jonah and Elijah, certain they had been the only ones willing to turn from idols. They would have rebuked Yahweh for having made the mistake of offering repentance to the Gentiles and now having to save them. They would have chafed against God's salvation of the Gentiles as hard as against his judgment of Jonah.

But could they have stood against the logic and love of Yahweh? Would they not now realize what it must mean to "be a blessing" and to be the people through whom "all peoples on earth will be blessed" (Gen. 12:2-3)? The covenant of Sinai had made them a "treasured possession" out of all nations (Ex. 19:5), but had not set aside the covenant with Abraham nor the fact that Yahweh God created *all* mankind: "the whole earth is mine" (Ex. 19:5, again).

The former Chief Rabbi of the British Empire writes: "The essential teaching is that the Gentiles *should not be grudged* God's love, care and forgiveness. It is this grudging which is so superbly rebuked throughout the Book."[1] If such was required of Israel under the Old Covenant, how much more to us under the New Covenant whose clear responsibility it is to "make disciples of all nations" (Matt. 28:19). Let us constantly monitor our relation to our God, to make certain we are not in need of repentance and are therefore willing to carry His good news as ministers of the New Covenant to all people—and every person!

1. J. H. Hertz, *The Pentateuch and Haftorahs*, p. 964.

NAHUM

NAHUM: INTRODUCTION

As mentioned in the General Introduction, Jonah is the best known of the prophets, whereas Nahum is among the least known. Both books are unique in relation to the other prophetic books (which are primarily declarations), but in very different ways: Jonah is a narrative, whereas Nahum is a dirge, a song celebrating the downfall of a foreign kingdom, with hardly a word directed toward Israel or Judah, as is normal with the other prophets.

NINEVEH AND THE LONGSUFFERING OF YAHWEH

Of course, Jonah and Nahum also share in common their exclusive focus on Nineveh, its role in the plan of God and its relation to the people of God. In Jonah, the gracious side of the longsuffering of Yahweh was expressed toward Nineveh. Given a warning and time to repent, the Ninevites did repent and Yahweh saved the city. In Nahum, however, the judgmental side of longsuffering—the fact that judgment is increased when people reject God's extended grace—is expressed toward Nineveh a century later. The Assyrians continued their wicked, inhuman, and expansionistic ways, and Yahweh destroyed them.

As in Jonah, Nahum based the righteous act of Yahweh in judging Nineveh on previous revelation, especially Exodus 34:6-7. Jonah focused on the compassionate forgiveness of verse 6, Nahum on the absolute justice of verse 7. (This will be developed further in the commentary on 1:2-3.)

DATE AND HISTORICITY

In contrast to Jonah, almost all scholars are agreed on Nahum's date and historicity. Two major world events frame the time of Nahum, the fall of Nineveh, of course, and the fall of Thebes ("No-amon," NASB) mentioned in 3:8-10. Thebes fell to the Assyrian king Ashubanipal in 663 B.C. and Nineveh fell in 612 B.C.

Nahum must have prophesied after 663 B.C. for his mention of the fall of Thebes to have significance. But he also must have prophesied before the fall of Nineveh, though not because he predicts it (remember, prophets were primarily "forth-tellers," not "foretellers"). Nahum could as easily be translated as a taunt following Nineveh's fall as a threat preceding it. But Nahum sees this fall from Judah's perspective as a liberation from oppression (1:15; 2:2), an oppression they would soon again experience at the hand of Babylon.[1] Thus a dating much later than 612 B.C. is suggested by very few interpreters.

The last great king of Assyria was Ashurbanipal, who died in 627 B.C. The history of Assyria for the next fifteen years was one of chaos and decline. Also in this era, the reforms of Josiah (2 Kings 23:1-25; 2 Chron. 34), especially following the discovery of the Book of the Law (c. 621 B.C.), led Judah to an unparalleled spiritual "high." This might have been responsible for Nahum's total lack of criticism of his own people, a perspective unique for a pre-exilic prophet. Thus most date Nahum around 615 B.C., though some see it as earlier, others later.[2] Fortunately, the message does not change based on the exact dating.

Most scholars feel very certain about the historical accuracy of Nahum—another strong contrast to Jonah. For the most part, their confidence is based on the remarkable parallels of Nahum's detailed descriptions with both ancient

1. John Merlin Powis Smith, "A Commentary on Nahum," p. 275.
2. Walter A. Maier, *The Book of Nahum,* pp. 27-40.

secular records of Nineveh's fall and contemporary archaeological discoveries—a luxury Jonah does not (yet?) enjoy.

The Babylonian Chronicle recorded Nineveh's last gasp:

> (In the fourteenth year) the king of Babylonia called out his army and marched to . . . the king of the Umman-manda and the king of Babylonia met each other in . . . Kyaxares made . . . the king of Babylonia to cross and they marched along the Tigris river bank and pitched camp by Nineveh. From the month of Sivan to the month of Ab they (advanced?) only three. . . . They made a strong attack on the citadel and in the month of Ab, [on the . . . th day the city was taken and] a great defeat inflicted on the people and (their) chiefs. On that same day Sin-shar-ishkun, the Assyrian king, [perished in the flames]. They carried off much spoil from the city and temple-area and turned the city into a ruin-mound and heap of debris . . .[3]

Greek historical sources, which claimed access to Persian records, add that heavy rains caused the river to rise and destroy the great walls of the city, and that the king killed himself in a great fire.[4] All records corroborate Nahum's description of Nineveh without generating any conflict.

Thus, most commentators write very positively and forcefully of Nahum's oracle as a historical document. (Some, however, have doubts about its abiding spiritual value.)[5]

UNITY

As in the case of Jonah's psalm (see notes on Jonah 2:2-9), much critical study of the past century has centered on the poem that opens Nahum's oracle (1:2-8). Since the late nineteenth century, scholars have debated the nature of the psalm,

3. D. W. Thomas, ed., *Documents from Old Testament Times,* p. 76. Also quoted in Ralph L. Smith, *Micah-Malachi,* p. 64.
4. Maier, pp. 109-10.
5. E.g., Charles L. Taylor, "The Book of Nahum," p. 954.

some assuming it to be an "acrostic," in which each line begins with the next letter of Hebrew alphabet. But since each letter is not represented and the lines are not in strict alphabetical order, these scholars must resort to much re-arrangement of the text to recreate the assumed original psalm that Nahum or a later editor used.[6]

Most commentators today agree that such reconstruction is arbitrary and subjective, especially in light of recent dis-coveries of very ancient Hebrew and Greek texts of Nahum practically identical to the traditional text.[7] Nahum and Jonah may have drawn on earlier resources that praised the attributes and actions of Yahweh in order to give their writing a traditional and biblical orientation. This is certainly true of Nahum's allusions to Exodus 20:5 and 34:6-7. But they freely adapted these materials to emphasize the thrust of their message.

The text of Nahum makes good sense as it is, as the com-mentary will develop, and is best left in the condition in which it has been transmitted for the past 2000 years.

NAHUM THE MAN

Less is known about Nahum than almost any other proph-et. All we know of him is gained from verse 1 and from the content and style of his writing. That he was an "Elkoshite" is not very helpful. Some understand it as a family name, though most understand it as his birthplace. But there is also no consensus on the location of Elkosh.

Some identify it with Capernaum, "village of Nahum," on the Sea of Galilee. Others locate Elkosh near Nineveh itself. Many believe Elkosh to be modern Beit-jibrin, a town about twenty-five miles southwest of Jerusalem. All are conjectures, though the exile and depopulation of Israel in Nahum's day

---

6. E.g., Taylor, p. 955.
7. Ralph L. Smith, p. 67.

and Nahum's references to Judah could favor, if any, Beit-jibrin.[8]

The name *Nahum* means "comfort" or "consolation." Certainly, Nahum is a book of comfort to Judah and all those oppressed by Assyria. In fact, following the parallel to 1:15 in Isaiah 52:7, the messenger brought Zion the joyful news that "Yahweh has *comforted* his people" (Isa. 52:9). A stark contrast is brought out within the book of Nahum: Judah has Nahum (1:1); Nineveh has no "Nahums" ("comforters" [NASB], 3:7). This does not necessarily mean the prophet is using a pseudonym or that his name was changed to fit the message, but rather that God chose a spokesman whose name suited the essence of His communication—as in the case with Jonah (see Jonah: Introduction).

Many see Nahum as "a representative of the old, narrow and shallow prophetism . . . the so-called 'false prophets' in general,"[9] because he does not lament over and criticize Judah for her idolatry and sins, but cares only that Yahweh has avenged His covenant people against an ancient foe. This is paralleled only by Obadiah, as far as an entire book is concerned. But besides the possibility that Nahum wrote in the great days of Josiah's reforms (see "Date," above), we should not expect all of the prophets to have the same message.

Nahum's contribution is his vision of Yahweh's justice in seeking out and destroying a wicked oppressor, not just because of her atrocities in Judah (1:12-13, 15), but because the whole world had felt her endless cruelty (3:19). As Jonah proclaimed Yahweh the Savior of all who repent, Nahum proclaimed Him as the Avenger of all who are oppressed.

Nahum, then, was a godly man who, like Jonah, was raised on the law and praise of Yahweh (1:2-8), but did not limit the application of Yahweh's character to the benefit of Israel and

8. John Merlin Powis Smith, pp. 286-87.
9. Ibid., p. 281.

Judah. He lamented world injustice, not just cruelty to his own people, and with perceptive observation and brilliant imagery proclaimed to the world the just death sentence Yahweh brought upon the cruelest civilization then known.

THE MESSAGE OF NAHUM FOR TODAY

Nahum's message is simple and clear, though thoroughly developed. Based on the eternal characteristics of Yahweh's longsuffering and justice (1:2-3), Nahum proclaims that the people of Nineveh will be crushed as they have crushed their fellows.

This judgment is Yahweh's just sentence against the guilt of the Ninevites (1:3): their drunken and evil plots against Him (1:9-11), their vile idolatry (1:14; 3:4), their devouring of other nations (2:11—3:1), and their inhuman actions in their conquests (3:10, 19). It is also a message of comfort and salvation to Judah (1:12-13, 15; 2:2) and to all who felt Assyria's "endless cruelty" (3:19).

Many commentators have undervalued Nahum's oracle as "fall[ing] below the standards set by the developed Judaeo-Christian tradition concerning the nature of God and man's relation with his brother man."[10] This criticism is supposedly based on the principle of love and forgiveness taught in the New Testament, and is frequently directed at the so-called imprecatory Psalms (e.g., Ps. 137).

But such a view of love and forgiveness accepts Exodus 34:6 and not 34:7. Yahweh *cannot* let the guilty go unpunished. Love that simply forgives is sentimentality. On the other hand, justice that does not allow for forgiveness is not known in the Scriptures. Those who experience Yahweh's forgiveness praise Him for His undeserved favor (Ps. 32; Jonah 2). Those who anticipate Yahweh's avenging of wrong done to them praise Him no less (Ps. 52). Yahweh does indeed

10. Taylor, p. 954.

show His "unfailing love" (Ps. 52:8) for those who love Him when He punishes their oppressors.

Man's inhumanity to man did not stop with Nineveh; nor did Yahweh's judgment on the oppressors. The martyrs under the altar in Revelation 6:9-11 saw no conflict between the New Testament revelation of the character of God and that revealed in Nahum. C. S. Lewis, who wrestled intensely with the imprecatory Psalms, finally concluded "if we look at their railings we find they are usually angry not simply because these things have been done to them but because these things are manifestly wrong, are hateful to God as well as to the victim."[11]

Yahweh established very early the principle that "whoever sheds the blood of man, by man shall his blood be shed" (Gen. 9:6) for all of humanity. For His people, He decreed that "I will bless those who bless you, and whoever curses you I will curse" (Gen. 12:3). Nahum voices the praise of Israel and the nations to the God who enforced these covenants in relation to cruel Nineveh, "the city of blood."

OUTLINE

I. Superscription, 1:1.
II. The Character of Yahweh Focused on Nineveh and Judah, 1:1-15.
   A. The Character of Yahweh Described, 1:2-8.
      a.1. Yahweh Avenges in Anger, 2-6.
         b. Yahweh Protects in Goodness, 7.
      a.2. Yahweh Destroys His Foes, 8.
   B. Yahweh's Character Focused, 1:9-15.
      a.1. (Nineveh) To Be Destroyed for Evil Plots, 9-11.
         b.1. (Judah) To Be Emancipated, 12-13.
      a.2. (Nineveh) To Be Destroyed for Idolatry, 14.
         b.2. Judah to Celebrate Festivals in Peace, 15.

11. C. S. Lewis, *Reflections on the Psalms* (New York: Harcourt, Brace & World, 1958), p. 30.

II. The Judgment of Nineveh Detailed, 2:1-13.
    A. The Attack of Nineveh Detailed, 2:1, 3-10.
    B. Yahweh Will Restore Jacob and Israel, 2:2.
    C. Nineveh Taunted in Defeat, 2:11-13.
IV. Woe to Nineveh! 3:1-19.
    A. Nineveh Is Justly Overthrown; Without Comforters,
       3:1-7.
    B. Nineveh Is Overthrown as She Overthrew Thebes,
       3:8-12.
    C. Failure of Defenses Mocked, 3:13-17.
    D. The World Rejoices over Nineveh's End, 3:18-19.

5

THE CHARACTER OF YAHWEH
FOCUSED ON NINEVEH AND JUDAH

(NAHUM 1:1-15)

SUPERSCRIPTION (1:1)

The opening of Nahum introduces us to an oracle, a place, a book, and a prophet. An "oracle" (*maśśā'* [1421e]) is a prophetic announcement of judgment, usually against the nations (Isa. 13:1; 15:1; 17:1; 19:1; etc.) but sometimes against Israel (Isa. 22:1; Mal. 1:1). Some interpreters relate its root concept to the simple idea of "lifting up the voice," whereas others see it as indicating the "burden" of judgment laid on the object of the oracle.[1] Regardless of derivation, it spells bad news for Nineveh.

Oracles and prophecies against Assyria in general and Nineveh in particular captured the attention of many of the pre-exilic prophets (Isa. 10:5-19; 14:24-27; 30:27-33; Mic. 5:5-6; Zeph. 2:13-14). None, however, were so captivated by the absolute justice of Nineveh's destruction and its implications for Israel and Judah as Nahum.

The place, Nineveh, was the capital of the powerful and ruthless Assyrian empire in the days of Nahum. The city existed in the days of Abraham (early 2d millennium B.C.), but came into prominence with the re-emergence of Assyria as a world power under Shalmaneser I (1274-1245 B.C.). Tiglath-pileser I (1114-1076 B.C.) established Nineveh as an alternate royal residence to Asshur and Calah. Ashurnasirpal II

---

1. For "lifting up the voice," see Ralph L. Smith, *Micah-Malachi,* p. 71. For "burden," see Walter A. Maier, *The Book of Nahum,* pp. 143, 146.

(883-859 B.C.) and Sargon II (722-705 B.C.)—the conqueror of Samaria and the Northern Kingdom—both had palaces there.

Sennacherib (705-681 B.C.) greatly expanded and fortified the city, making it his primary residence. One of his major accomplishments was the building of a canal and dam on the River Gomel, north of Nineveh, to control the waters of the Khasr River, which flowed through Nineveh. With the Tigris as a natural "moat" to the west and the Khasr to provide water, Nineveh was confident of her unassailable position. Sennacherib invaded Judah in 701 B.C., destroying many smaller cities, but not capturing Jerusalem (2 Kings 18:13—19:36). The temple of Nisroch, in which he was assassinated (2 Kings 19:37), may have been in Nineveh.[2]

The last great king of Assyria was Ashurbanipal (669-627 B.C.). He ruled the vast Assyrian empire from Nineveh, a time during which the city must have felt invulnerable. But within fifteen years of his death the city was a smoldering ruin.

Descriptions of their conquests, killings, and subjugation of nations,[3] and even their artwork, which shows decapitation, dismemberment, impaling, skinning alive, and other atrocities, show that the Assyrians were precisely the cruel and pompous creatures Nahum describes. Their end satisfied the justice of Yahweh and the cries for vengeance of Israel and Judah, as well as those of the known world.

"The book of the vision" is a label unique to Nahum. Most prophetic oracles were verbal. Nahum's appears to have been literature from the beginning. The word "vision" (*ḥāzôn* [633a]) is related to a major designation for and function of the prophet as a "seer" (see General Introduction). It underlines the revelatory nature of Nahum's "oracle" and "book," and is also used to introduce Isaiah (1:1) and Obadiah (1).

"Nahum" means "comfort" or "consolation" (Isa. 40:1; 52:9). His message of Nineveh's end brings "comfort" to

---

2. J. D. Douglas, ed., *New Bible Dictionary,* s. v. "Nineveh."
3. D. W. Thomas, ed., *Documents from Old Testament Times,* pp. 46-74.

Judah (1:12-13, 15; 2:2), but leaves Nineveh without "comforters" (3:7, NASB). (On the person of Nahum and the location of Elkosh, see the Introduction.)

THE CHARACTER OF YAHWEH DESCRIBED (1:2-8)

This introductory poem describes the specific characteristics of Yahweh that will be focused on Nineveh (just wrath) and on Judah and Israel (deliverance and protection).

Several of the lines start with successive letters of the Hebrew alphabet, and for a while scholars attempted to reconstruct the assumed original acrostic poem (Pss. 111; 112; 119). Though verses 2-8 may have been adapted from an acrostic psalm praising Yahweh's avenging wrath, it is impossible to recreate the "original" without badly damaging the text of Nahum. This is especially true of the key allusions to Exodus 20:5 and 34:6-7, which would have to be left out all together.[4]

YAHWEH AVENGES IN ANGER (1:6)

Yahweh was first described as a "jealous God" in Exodus 20:5 in the context of idolatry (cf. 34:14; Deut. 4:24; 5:9; 6:15; Josh. 24:19). He demands exclusive worship. This characteristic, then, might apply to 1:14, where Nineveh is said to be destroyed for her vile idolatry, or for her competing with Yahweh as Judah's master.

But the word and its cognates (*qānā'* [2038]) can also mean "to be zealous for," thus "defend the honor of." This was the case in relation to Phinehas (Num. 25:11-13) and Elijah (1 Kings 19:10, 14), where their actions were determined by their zealous desire for Yahweh's honor. Yahweh, too, can be zealous for His people, and thus restore them from judgment (Joel 2:18; Zech. 1:14; 8:2). Perhaps both nuances are here, jealous judgment of Nineveh and zealous restoration of Israel and Judah.

---

4. Charles L. Taylor, "The Book of Nahum," p. 955; see also the NEB.

Three times in verse 2 we read of Yahweh's "vengeance" (*nāqam* [1413]). The term does not mean that God is selfishly getting even. Rather, He judicially punishes those who hate Him and their fellow human beings, whether Israel (Deut. 32:35) or the nations (34:43). Yahweh brought upon Nineveh the death sentence of the Noahic Covenant (Gen. 9:6) and the curse of the Abrahamic Covenant (Gen. 12:3) for their endless cruelties.

Yahweh is "filled with wrath." This is one of five different words used for "anger," and is repeated with three others in verse 6. He "maintains His wrath" as well. In the other occurences of this word in relation to anger (*nāṭar* [1356]), Israelites were commanded *not* to maintain anger against their fellows (Lev. 19:18), and Yahweh was praised because He *did not* "harbor his anger forever" (Ps. 103:9; Jer. 3:5, 12). Only against His "foes," His "enemies," those who hate and oppose him, does Yahweh maintain His wrath.

"Yahweh is slow to anger" (v. 3). What a contrast! Or is it? At first glance, we wonder why the sudden change. But, remembering that this line appears in Exodus 34:6-7, we recall that the longsuffering of Yahweh is both gracious and judgmental. In Jonah, that Yahweh was "slow to anger" meant that He relented (*nāḥam,* by the way!) when Nineveh repented (4:2). In Nahum, though Yahweh is still "slow to anger," He has now *become* angry—Nineveh has no more time.

Thus, instead of "abounding in love and faithfulness," Yahweh is "great [abounds] in power" (cf. Isa. 63:1-6). Exodus 34:6 is no longer in focus; it is time for 34:7. "He will not leave the guilty unpunished" is an exact quote of this verse. And, as Jonah had boldly applied the compassion and grace of God to Nineveh in the eighth century, Nahum applies the righteous, avenging wrath of God to Nineveh in the seventh century. Yahweh's grace is not limited to Israel; nor is His judgment.

As Jonah pictured God as both the covenant God of Israel

and the God of all creation, so Nahum turned to creation imagery in verses 3*b*-5. We recall from Jonah (1:4-16) that "His way is in the whirlwind and the storm." Appearances of God (theophanies) are often accompanied by such cataclysmic imagery, as though creation itself bolts and runs in abject terror when the Creator manifests Himself (Ex. 19:16-18; Ps. 18:7-10; Hab. 3:3-15; Zech. 7:14).

Yahweh rides or walks on the clouds (2 Sam. 22:10; Ps. 68:4; 104:3). This is a favorite Canaanite description of the god Baal as well.[5] But whereas Baal had to fight continually against his great enemy Yamm, the sea, Yahweh simply "rebukes the sea and it dries up." Hebrew poets often use the terminology of pagan hymnody (as the church has always borrowed contemporary musical concepts), but they always turn it against the "gods," to rebuke those originally praised.

Drying the sea and the rivers recalls the bringing of land from the domination of the sea in Genesis 1:9-10 (cf. Job 38:8-11). It also definitely speaks of Yahweh's salvation of Israel at the Red Sea (Ex. 14; 15:8) and His bringing them into the land through the Jordan (Josh. 3; cf. Ps. 114:3-4).

Bashan, Carmel, and Lebanon were regions famous for their mountainous heights and lush vegetation (Ps. 68:15-16; Isa. 10:34; 35:2). But if the depths of the sea could not withstand Yahweh, neither could the high places of the earth.

The quaking and trembling of verse 5 again recalls the theophany at Sinai (Ex. 19:18; Ps. 114:3-4). At the presence of Yahweh, the hills "melt away." This word is repeated in 2:7, where "the palace collapses" ("is dissolved," NASB) at the onslaught of the river. Because the earth "trembles at his presence," its "inhabitants" tremble as well, once again recalling the theophany at Sinai (Ex. 19:18; 20:18; Ps. 114:7-8).

Four words for anger are used in verse 6, which rhetorically asks, "What nation can withstand the God who overcame the

5. Ralph L. Smith, p. 74.

primordial chaos?"[6] "Indignation" (*za'am* [568a]) is also rendered "curse" (Num. 23:7-8) and might imply the wrath of Yahweh that stems from the curse of the Abrahamic Covenant. The "fierce anger" of Yahweh was avoided in Jonah 3:8-9 when the Ninevites turned from their wicked ways. But now, having rededicated themselves to abominations, there is no escaping it.

"Jealousy" and "fiery wrath" are connected in Deuteronomy 4:24 and 32:21-22, and this connection was graphically seen in front of the Tabernacle in Leviticus 10:1-2. Elijah experienced a wind that shattered rocks, an earthquake in the mountains, and a devastating fire; but found Yahweh in a gentle whisper (1 Kings 19:11-13). But Yahweh is not whispering to Nineveh.

YAHWEH PROTECTS IN GOODNESS (1:7)

In dramatic contrast (and chiastic construction, see outline in introduction to Jonah) to what precedes and follows, "Yahweh is good." Yahweh is praised for His goodness more than for any other attribute, at least two dozen times in the Psalms alone (e.g., 25:7; 34:8; 118:1, 29). Yahweh is good and does good (Ps. 119:68), but only those who are good experience His goodness.

Though a strongly positive word, "good" is abstract and is often specified by another term, such as "love" (*ḥesed,* Ps. 136:1). Here Yahweh's goodness is seen in His care "for those who trust him." Yahweh as "refuge" is another theme of the Psalms (27:1; 28:8; 31:2-4; etc.), a dramatic contrast to Nineveh's failure to find "refuge" from her enemies (3:11). The "times of trouble" could be rendered the "day of the foe," to point out the relation of this word to verse 2. Yahweh shelters those who trust or take refuge in Him (25 times in the Psalms, e.g., 18:2; Prov. 30:5), saving them from distress in general and the foe in particular.

6. Brevard S. Childs, *Introduction to the Old Testament as Scripture,* p. 444.

YAHWEH DESTROYS HIS FOES (1:8)

The psalm returns to judgment, paralleling verses 2-6. By dramatic contrast to verse 7, where Yahweh is a refuge to those who trust Him (where "floods" cannot reach, Ps. 32:6), Yahweh is now a "flood" to His foes (cf. Dan. 9:26; 11:22). Though not the same word as in Genesis 6-9, the concept is obviously the same as the great flood and the flood at the Red Sea (Ex. 14-25). It could also graphically anticipate the destruction of Nineveh by flooding (2:6).

"Nineveh" is in half brackets in the *New International Version* because the word is supplied by the translators. The *New American Standard Bible* reads more formally, "its [her] site," which most likely refers "to Nineveh or her patron goddess, Ishtar."[7]

The parallel lines "he will make an end of [Nineveh];/he will pursue his foes ['enemies,' v. 2] into darkness" describe the absolute destruction Yahweh brings on His enemies. For "darkness" is separation from God, total helplessness, utter defeat (Job 5:12-14; Prov. 20:20; Isa. 8:20-22).

YAHWEH'S CHARACTER FOCUSED (1:9-15)

The preceding poem was a forceful, though general, description of Yahweh's good protection of His people and righteous vengeance against His foes (though the NIV had directly applied the latter to Nineveh on the basis of verse 1). The rest of the chapter does indeed apply the poem to Nineveh and Judah, though not by name but by pronoun ("you"). (The NIV, TEV, LB, and JB [margin] make clear these applications.)

(NINEVEH) TO BE DESTROYED FOR EVIL PLOTS (1:9-11)

The first verse directly connects this section to the preceding poem with the phrase "he will bring to an end" (cf.

7. Ralph L. Smith, p. 75.

v. 8) and the word "trouble" (cf. v. 7; cf. "foes," v. 2).

This short section is also framed by the concept of plotting against Yahweh (vv. 9, 11). This immediately brings to mind the imagery of Psalm 2, where plots and warfare against Israel are, in cosmic reality, against Yahweh the God of Israel (Ps. 2:1-2). And, as these plots are ultimately destined to fail (Ps. 2:8-9), so now in relation to Nineveh.

"Trouble will not come a second time" might be an assurance to Judah that they will never again face devastation by Assyria as they had in 701 B.C. at the hand of Sennacherib.[8] However, as it parallels "he will bring to an end," it more likely simply reinforces the utter destruction of Nineveh.

Three images in verse 10 describe their end. Some versions (RSV, NEB, TEV, and JB) eliminate the "drunk" image as very difficult and confused Hebrew.[9] But the three lines together can form an intelligible picture: The Ninevites, incapacitated and immobile as those captured by thorns or drink (cf. 3:11), would be consumed as fully as chaff by fire.

The one "who plots evil" (v. 11) is probably the king of Assyria (cf. LB). The *Jerusalem Bible* has rendered the last line "a man with the mind of Belial," thus personifying the word (*beliya'al* [246g]) as a demonic or satanic being, as in later Jewish literature and 2 Corinthians 6:15.[10] But as it is paired with "evil," a word never personified, the traditional rendering "wicked" or "worthless" (Judg. 19:22; 1 Sam. 2:12; 25:25) is preferred.

(JUDAH) TO BE EMANCIPATED (1:12-13)

The *New English Bible* has radically rearranged this section, including transposing verse 12 after 15, in order to "recover" the acrostic and group all like prophecies together. But as the text stands, it alternates nicely between Assyria (vv.

---

8. Maier, pp. 184-85.
9. See John Merlin Powis Smith, p. 301.
10. Maier, pp. 199-200.

9-11, 14) and Judah (vv. 12-13, 15) as did the poem.

The content of these verses prompts the *New International Version* to include "O Judah" in half brackets, especially since the name does appear in verse 15. "This is what Yahweh says," the famous "Thus saith the LORD" of the King James Version, is a phrase often used to indicate an announcement by Yahweh (e.g., Amos 1:3, 6, 9, 11, 13). But this is its only occurrence in Nahum. It serves to emphasize the change in tone from terrifying judgment to joyful deliverance.

"Unscathed" could also be translated "at peace" (*shālēm* [2401]). Nineveh was whole and at peace, whereas those under the iron fist of her reign of terror were fragmented and in bondage. But Yahweh would turn her peace to destruction, thus bringing peace (*shālôm* [2401a], v. 15) to Judah. "Pass away" is the same word that described the "overwhelming" flood of verse 8. Thus, the oracle of Judah's salvation is connected to both the poem preceding and second oracle following.

As "trouble will not come a second time" in verse 9, so Yahweh's affliction at the hand of Nineveh will not come again. This is similar to Isaiah 40:1-2, when Yahweh calls His people out of Babylon, proclaiming their "comfort" and the end of their "hard service." Both Assyria and Babylon were instruments of Yahweh's judgment on Israel, but the oppressor would not escape His just destruction (Hab. 2:2-20).

Judah's emancipation from Assyrian bondage is pictured in the parallel metaphors, "break their yoke from your neck/and tear your shackles away." The "yoke" is a common image of defeat and captivity (Isa. 58:6; Jer. 27:1—28:14), although shackles were more often the actual implement of bondage (Judg. 16:21; 2 Kings 25:7). The sum total of the metaphors: "Judah will be freed from a century's oppression!"

(NINEVEH) TO BE DESTROYED FOR IDOLATRY (1:14)

In verses 9-11, Nineveh had been condemned for "evil plots" against Yahweh. Now she is condemned for her evil actions against Yahweh—her idolatry.

Once again, Yahweh addresses "you," which some take as the king of Nineveh in particular (JB [margin]; LB).[11] Yahweh has "given a command" for his end (Isa. 23:11; Jer. 47:7) as He "says" or proclaims the freeing of His people (v. 12).

"You will have no descendants to bear your name" parallels "I will prepare your grave." Both speak of the utter decimation of Nineveh and/or her king, as opposed to Abraham, for example, who was still producing many nations on his deathbed (Gen. 25:1-10).

Framed by these death sentences is the reason: idolatry. Three different words are used to point out that in multiplying their objects of worship, the Ninevites still missed the one true God. Because they cut Him out of their pantheon, Yahweh will "cut off" their idols and "cut off" Nineveh (1:15; 2:13; cf. 3:15, NASB).

The word "vile" is the same as "lighten" in Jonah 1:5 (*qālal* [2028]). The word is used of treating someone lightly or with spite (Gen. 16:4-5) and can intensify to mean "curse," as in Genesis 12:3. Once again, there is an intimation that Yahweh is "cursing" Nineveh for her cursing of His people.

JUDAH TO CELEBRATE FESTIVALS IN PEACE (1:15)

The final verse of chapter 1 in English is the first verse of chapter 2 in Hebrew (cf. JB; NJV). It is the second salvation oracle to Judah, this time addressed by name.

The image of the messenger on the mountains, "bring[ing] good news," and "proclaim[ing] peace," is also in Isaiah 52:7 (cf. 40:9). Those who date Isaiah 40-66 to the post-exilic period assume "deutero-Isaiah" borrowed from Nahum; conservatives assume the opposite. Regardless, the image of the messenger is an old one. He can be "one who brings good news" (2 Sam. 18:31; 1 Kings 1:42) or bad (1 Sam. 4:17). Here, as in Isaiah, the news is good: "peace" for God's peo-

11. Ralph L. Smith, pp. 78-79.

ple because there is no more "peace" for the oppressor (1:12).

Because "peace" is here, Judah can "fulfill" her "vows." Both "peace" and "fulfill" come from the same root (*shālēm* [2401]), and Nahum the poet takes advantage of the happy coincidence of terminology to play with the words. In Joel, Yahweh had sent a locust plague to strip the land bare so His people would learn what it felt like not to receive their due from the land (1:5, 11-12, 16a, 18; cf. 1:9, 13, 16b). Similarly, Nineveh had stripped the land by war and tribute. But now, with the coming of peace, tribute can be restored to Yahweh, the festivals celebrated, vows fulfilled.

"Peace" connects this salvation oracle to the previous one by way of contrast to Nineveh. "Wicked" ("Belial," JB) also joins it to the first judgment threat of verses 9-11. This section, which ends chapter 1 (or begins chapter 2), is also connected to the end of chapter 2 by contrast to Nineveh. For though the herald is seen and heard on the mountains of Israel, "the voices of your [Nineveh's] messengers will no longer be heard" (2:13).

6

THE JUDGMENT OF NINEVEH DETAILED

(NAHUM 2:1-13)

THE ATTACK OF NINEVEH DETAILED (2:1, 3-10)

Chapter 2 continues in the same style as chapter 1 ended: the first two verses alternate between Nineveh's end and Judah's rebirth. The *New English* and *Jerusalem* bibles have moved verse 2 to follow 1:15. However, verse 1 begins the *detailed* account of the fall of Nineveh, though still addressed as "you." Thus, our outline places 2:1-2 in this section, though it could be the end of the previous section, as:

a.3. The Attack of Nineveh Detailed, 2:1
b.3. Yahweh Will Restore Jacob, 2:2

The detailing of Nineveh's fall begins with the announcement of the attack. The ancient attributes of God revealed in 1:2-8 and their focus as the judgment threats of 1:9-11 and 14 are now being realized. Nineveh the attacker is now the attacked! The four lines that follow also begin Nahum's concise and muscular poetic style, which forcefully drove his message home in his day and has won the admiration of scholars for the millennia that have followed.

Because these descriptions are self-evident, from this point on the commentary will only point out key words, images, and cultural insights not apparent in the words themselves. Those desiring more details can, of course, consult the fuller treatments of Walter A. Maier and Ralph L. Smith (see Bibliography).

The first lines mockingly call Nineveh to defend herself. The last two lines fascinatingly reflect previously used vocabulary. The two words translated "brace" and "marshal" are the very words rendered "be strong and courageous" in Deuteronomy (31:6, 7, 23) and Joshua (1:6, 7, 9, 18; 10:25). As an inside joke to the Israelites, Nahum taunts the residents of Nineveh to prepare themselves to fight against Yahweh as Israel had prepared herself to fight on His side! They need to "marshal [much] strength," for they are about to face the God who is "great in strength" ("power," 1:3).

YAHWEH WILL RESTORE JACOB AND ISRAEL (2:2)

In this final word specifically directed to Jacob and Israel, we complete the picture of the restoration of God's people. In 1:12-13, they heard the message that they would be freed from oppression. In 1:15, "peace," "celebrate," and "fulfill" were key terms. Now, they heard that their "splendor," the produce of the land, will be restored just as Joel (2:18-27) had promised following the locust plague.

Some alter the word "splendor" to "vine" with the change of a single letter,[1] thus creating a nice parallel to the latter two lines of the verse. But this is no more necessary than "recovering" the acrostic poem of chapter 1. Maier, on the other hand, understands the verse not as restoration, but as a reason for judging Nineveh: "Because Yahweh hath cut off the pride of Jacob,/As the pride of Israel." But this also is idiosyncratic, though well defended.[2]

THE ATTACK OF NINEVEH DETAILED (2:3-10) (CONTINUED)

THE ATTACKER ADVANCES (3-4)

The attacking armies were brilliantly clothed, well prepared, organized, and awesome. By contrast (5a), the "picked troops" of Nineveh "stumble on their way" to the

1. JB; John Merlin Powis Smith, "A Commentary on Nahum," p. 305.
2. Walter A. Maier, *The Book of Nahum,* pp. 227-35.

defense. "Red" or "scarlet" seems to have been the characteristic color of the Babylonians (Ezek. 22:14), though some have seen the clothing and shields as reddened by blood or reflection.[3]

Also catching the eye were the fiery reflections from the armored chariots, not from knife blades on the wheels,[4] and red "cypress" or "pine" spears. Some versions emend the Hebrew word for "pine" to "horses" (RSV, JB, NEB, TEV, following the Septuagint and Syriac). Again, the Hebrew makes sense and need not be altered.

NINEVEH'S DEFENDERS FALTER (5a)

"He summons" etc. can be understood as referring to the king of Assyria (NIV, TEV).[5] Other translations (JB, NEB, and NJV) see it as continuing the description of the attackers.[6] The former would read "they stumble on their way" as a contrast to the ordered movement of the attackers, perhaps because of drunkenness (3:11). The latter understand the stumbling as falling over each other as they press the attack to the wall.

THE ATTACKER PREVAILS (5b-10)

Most, if not all, understand the second half of verse 5 as referring to the attackers. "The protective shield" is probably a "wheeled shelter . . . to protect the crews that swung the battering rams" (NJV) from the arrows and other missiles that would rain down upon them from the walls.

However it was not the battering ram but Nineveh's protective river that overthrew the city. Most of Nineveh's city gates faced the Tigris and its canal. But it was probably not these "river gates" that were thrown open, but an "over-

3. Maier, pp. 236-38.
4. John Merlin Powis Smith, p. 314.
5. Ralph L. Smith, *Micah-Malachi*, p. 81.
6. John Merlin Powis Smith, pp. 316-17.

whelming flood'' (cf. 1:8) of the Khasr River. Sennacherib (705-681 B.C.) had built a system of dams to control the seasonal flooding of the rivers that ran by and through Nineveh. Traces of the gates that controlled the water flow have been recovered by archaeologists.[7]

Apparently the invading armies closed the gates of the Khasr, initially to cut off Nineveh's water supply, and later opened these gates to release a short-lived but violently destructive flood. This would accord with the Greek traditions perpetuated by Diodorus and Xenophon.[8]

As a result, ''the palace collapses,'' or ''dissolves'' (NASB) before the flood. The metaphor of 1:5 has become literal in relation to Nineveh.

The first word of verse 7 is extremely difficult to translate. Some (NIV and NKJV) read it as a verb, ''it is decreed,'' though most versions read it as a noun, the proper name ''Huzzab'' (KJV, NJV), or the ''Queen,'' ''Lady,'' or ''Mistress'' of the city.[9] Whether the Queen, the goddess Zib, or Nineveh herself, the picture of defeat is just as humiliating and shameful.

She is ''exiled and carried away.'' These same terms could be rendered ''stripped and made to ascend,'' referring to the queen's public humiliation and her climbing on to the funeral pyre in which tradition tells us the king and all his concubines perished (see ''Date and History'' section of the introduction to Nahum).[10] Either option continues the graphic picture of Nineveh's humbling in defeat, while ''the slave girls moan like doves/and beat upon their breasts,'' wildly lamenting the death throes of their mistress or city.

Verse 9 continues the imagery of Nineveh flooded by the waters of the Khasr, now losing its water and its inhabitants.[11]

7. Maier, p. 253.
8. For a contrary opinion, see John Merlin Powis Smith, pp. 318-20.
9. Maier, pp. 256-57.
10. Ibid., p. 257.
11. Ralph L. Smith, p. 83.

Once both the waters and the soldiers had been her defense. Now, the leaders cry "Stop! Stop!"—but no one turns back.

Nahum invites the attackers to loot the city, as Isaiah had invited Assyria to loot Damascus and Samaria (Isa. 8:3-4). Ironically, the plunder of Nineveh is that which she had originally plundered herself!

The power of Nahum's poetry is seen in vigorous translations such as the *New International Version,* the *Jerusalem Bible,* and the *New English Bible.* The New Jewish Version beautifully captures the sound of verse 10 with "Desolation, devastation and destruction!" for the Hebrew *bu-ka, u-me-bu-ka, u-me-bul-la-ka.* The individual responses that complete the verse speak vividly and need no comment (cf. Josh. 2:9-11).

NINEVEH TAUNTED IN DEFEAT (2:11-13)

The metaphor of the lions' den in verses 11-12 is crystal clear in itself. It is eminently suited to Nineveh, for the lion was the symbol of the nation (cf. Hos. 5:13-14). Lions adorned their artwork, lions supplied the kings with their greatest sport, and lions were used as metaphors for the kings themselves.[12]

As lions filled Nineveh, Nahum fills these verses with eight occurences of three different terms for lion. The "lion" (Nineveh) once roamed among the nations, feeding, killing, and strangling prey. The "city of blood" (3:1) had grown fat and wealthy off the flesh and plunder of its victims, "with nothing to fear."

But that was in the past; where are they *now*? They are no more to be found because "Yahweh Almighty" is against them. "Almighty" follows the rendering of the Septuagint, as does Revelation 4:8. The term (*ṣeḇā'ôt* [1865b]), however, does not just refer to power but powers, that is, "armies." Thus most versions render, "Lord of Hosts." This title is a

12. Maier, p. 277.

favorite of Isaiah, who uses it more than 60 times. It emphasizes the power and sovereignty of Yahweh, who is in control of the heavenly (Isa. 6:3, 5) and earthly hosts (10:16-34). How appropriate an image to use for Yahweh, who has marshalled the forces of creation and Babylon against Nineveh!

The terrifying statement "I am against you!" (v. 13) is repeated in 3:5. In both places it explains why Nineveh's fall was so swift, so complete. The chariots that had flashed in the sun (3-4) now smoldered in the dust. The young lions who had devoured nations were now devoured by the sword. That Yahweh "cut off your prey from the land" (NASB) is a judgment on Nineveh, not the prey. Every other "cutting off" is directed at Nineveh (1:14-15; 3:15). We could paraphrase, "I will cut you off from snatching any more prey from the land."

"Declares" ($ne'\bar{u}m$ [1272a]) is our fifth term indicating Yahweh's revealing of Nahum's prophecy ("oracle" and "vision," 1:1; "says," 1:12; "command," 1:14). This word occurs 376 times in the Bible and is found in every prophet except Daniel, Jonah, and Habakkuk. "The root is used exclusively of divine speaking. Hence, its appearance calls special attention to the origin and authority of what is said" (TWOT, p. 541).

Verse 13 reiterates the realities and the metaphors of destruction found throughout the chapter. Israel's heralds were bringing "good news" of "peace" (1:15), but "the voices of your [Nineveh's] messengers will no longer be heard." Yahweh has worked to "silence the foe and the avenger" (Ps. 8:2).

7

WOE TO NINEVEH!

(NAHUM 3:1-19)

The final section of Nahum begins with a cry of "Woe!" The Hebrew word (*hôy* [485]), as its various English translations, represents the sound of shock and surprise, of disgust and disdain. The majority of its 51 appearances in the Bible are in prophetic utterances of doom and destruction (e.g., Isa. 5:8-22; Hab. 2:6-19; cf. Matt. 23:13-27).

NINEVEH IS JUSTLY OVERTHROWN; WITHOUT COMFORTERS
(3:1-7)

NINEVEH EARNS HER JUDGMENT (1-4)

Nineveh is decried as "the city of blood" (cf. Ezek. 22:2; 24:6, 9; Hab. 2:12). Walter Maier[1] quotes extensively from texts in which the Assyrians revel with glee in their slaughter of the nations, skinning men alive and decorating the walls with the skins, burning prisoners alive, dismembering, decapitating, blinding, and impaling men and women alike (cf. 3:10).

Verse 1 introduces the rest of the chapter, which details the Assyrians' "lies" (idolatry, 4), their "plunder," and their "victims" (2-3, 8-10). Verses 2-3 can be taken as an aside, continuing the narrative of Nineveh's fall,[2] or, more likely, as a description of Nineveh's own assaults against the nations over the centuries.[3]

---

1. Walter A. Maier, *The Book of Nahum,* pp. 291-92.
2. John Merlin Powis Smith, "A Commentary on Nahum," p. 336.
3. Ralph L. Smith, *Micah-Malachi,* p. 86.

The punching poetic style piles up images as Nineveh piled up plunder and victims. These verses echo 2:3-9, adding to the picture that as Nineveh treated the nations, so she will be treated (Gen. 9:6). Perhaps the most dramatic image is that of "stumbling." At her height, Nineveh stumbled over the piles of corpses of those she killed in her attacks (v. 3). In her fall, her troops stumble over themselves, the corpses-to-be, as they futilely man the defense (2:5).

"The wanton lust of a harlot" (v. 4) describes the reason for Assyria's aggressive cruelties. The *New Jewish Version* again captures Nahum's word plays:

> Because of the countless harlotries of the harlot,
>   The winsome mistress of sorcery,
> Who ensnared nations with her harlotries
>   And peoples with her sorcery.

The key words "harlot" and "sorcery" are used of the nations (Isa. 23:15-18; 47:9, 12) and Israel (Isa. 1:21; Ezek. 16:30-41) to describe deceitful practices of idolatry and unfaithfulness to Yahweh, usually in the context of judgment. The word rendered "enslaved" or "ensnared" is normally used of "selling" (*mākar* [1194]). In another ironic twist, Nahum pictures the harlot, who seduces others by selling herself, seducing others into being sold themselves as slaves (cf. Joel 3:3, 6, 8).

YAHWEH TURNS THE TABLES ON NINEVEH (5-7)

"Yahweh Almighty" again declares "I am against you" (2:13). Verses 5-7 (cf. comments on 2:7) picture Yahweh as the Conqueror exposing, humiliating, and treating Nineveh with the contempt she had shown the world for centuries (Isa. 20:2-4). (Unfortunately, these same images would soon be applied to decadent Judah [Jer. 13:22-27; Lam. 1:9]).

Picking up the cries and laments of Nineveh's allies and vassals (cf. Ps. 31:11; Ezek. 27:25-36), Yahweh taunts the bloody city, the cruel harlot. Yahweh, who found Nahum ("comfort") for His people, can find no "Nahums" (comforters) for Nineveh (cf. Isa. 51:19; Lam. 1:2-21).

NINEVEH IS OVERTHROWN AS SHE OVERTHREW THEBES (3:8-12)

THEBES, THE EXAMPLE OF DESTRUCTION (8-10)

Thebes was "the chief city of Upper [southern] Egypt and capital of Egypt during most of that nation's periods of political unity from the Middle Kingdom (c. 2000 B.C.) to the Assyrians' invasion under Ashurbanipal (c. 661 B.C.)."[4] Her strong position on the Nile (v. 8) was similar to Nineveh's position on the Tigris. Her destruction at the hand of Ashurbanipal became the pattern for Nineveh's decimation at the hand of Yahweh.

Thebes was a city of the gods (*No Amon* means "city of Amon" in Egyptian), filled with magnificent temples and monuments. Protected by 450 miles of desert, Egypt and Cush to the north, the Red Sea to the east, Ethiopia ("Put") to the south, and Libya to the east, she must have felt immensely secure.

But fall she did, to the ruthless Ashurbanipal in 663 B.C. Ralph L. Smith quotes the text in which the Assyrian recorded:

> I carried off from Thebes heavy booty, beyond counting. I made Egypt (Masur) and Nubia feel my weapons bitterly and celebrated my triumph. With full hands and safely, I returned to Nineveh, the city (where I exercise) my rule.[5]

Nahum records the human carnage: the captives exiled, the infants "dashed to pieces," the nobility enslaved. The Assyrians treated Thebes savagely, but Yahweh asks, "Are

---

4. George A. Buttrick, ed., *Interpreter's Dictionary of the Bible,* s.v. "Thebes."
5. Ralph L. Smith, p. 64.

you better?'' that is, ''Are you more secure?'' This mocks the attitude of the monarch quoted above. The answer, of course, is a resounding No!

NINEVEH ASSURED OF DESTRUCTION (11-12)

Nineveh "too will become drunk." This may be a metaphor for destruction (as in 1:10, cf. Jer. 25:27-29; Lam. 4:21; Ezek. 23:32-34), or a literal state of drunkenness, as in the Greek accounts (cf. comments on 2:5*a*).[6] Though they "will go into hiding/and seek refuge from the enemy," they will find no refuge, for only Yahweh is an adequate "refuge in times of trouble" (1:7).

Two further comparisons finish this taunt. The figure of fruit ripe for the picking is transparent to anyone who has been around fruit trees. Nineveh is ripe for judgment (cf. Amos 8:1-2). She will be consumed by those she had devoured.

The "troops" are called "women" because a female (who would not have been trained to fight in those days) could not possibly stand against a male warrior in hand-to-hand combat (cf. Isa. 19:16; Jer. 50:37; 51:30).

The resultant picture is of Nineveh, gates wide open, bars burned (so the gates could not be relocked, cf. Isa. 45:2; Jer. 51:30), naked to the world, and defenseless before her attackers.

FAILURE OF DEFENSES MOCKED (3:13-17)

A final satirical warning, similar to that of 2:1 but filled with a mixture of metaphors, precedes the song of rejoicing over Nineveh's total defeat.

As though the defenders could ever hope to rebuild the fifty-foot high walls of sun-dried clay brick that the Khasr had washed away, Nahum "commands" them to "draw water" to "work the clay,/tread the mortar,/repair the brick-

6. Maier, p. 109.

work!'' (v. 14). In the same breath, however, he proclaims their certain cutting down (v. 15; 1:14, 15; 2:13 NASB) by sword and fire.

Verses 15*b*-17 are built on a mixed and extended metaphor of the "locusts." First, sword and fire will consume Nineveh "like grasshoppers" consume vegetation (cf. Joel 1:4-7; Amos 7:1-2). The use of the image is then switched: Nineveh cannot escape locust-like devastation even if they "multiply like grasshoppers!"

This same application then turns to Nineveh's "merchants" (mercenaries). Though made numerous as locusts, even as "the stars of the sky" (Gen. 15:5; 22:17; etc.), they also act like locusts and shed their skin, (or "strip the land," NIV) and fly away.[7] The great number of Nineveh's allies are no help in her time of trouble. The mercenaries simply switch loyalties (as locusts shed their skin) and continue their business elsewhere (cf. Ezek. 27).

The image is used again as a simile of Nineveh's defenders: "Your guards are like locusts/your officials like swarms of locusts"—not because they were numerous or because they consumed their foes, but because they flew away at the first hint of trouble (cf. 2 Kings 25:1-5)! We have all seen insects on a wall in the early morning, immobilized by the cold. When warmed by the sun, they zip away to who knows where. So Nineveh, lulled into complacency by pride in her own strength, was now warmed by the heat of the siege and flew away.

THE WORLD REJOICES OVER NINEVEH'S END (3:18-19)

The king of Assyria is addressed directly for the first time, as the tone quiets and the metaphors change from locusts to shepherds and sheep. "Shepherds" is a regular designation for leaders in the Bible (Jer. 23:1-4; Ezek. 34); "slumber" and "rest" regularly mean death (Ps. 76:5; Jer. 51:39, 57).

7. Ralph L. Smith, p. 90.

Nineveh's "picked troops," who had stumbled to the defense (2:5), are now the "nobles" who sleep in death. As a result the "people are scattered on the mountains" (v. 18) "like sheep without a shepherd" (1 Kings 22:17; cf. Num. 27:17; Isa. 13:14).

Lest the king hold out any hope, he is told he is terminally ill, without hope of healing (cf. Jer. 6:14; 8:11, 22). But his grief is the joy of the world, his death sentence is their pardon. Upon hearing the "news" about Nineveh (cf. 1:15), everyone "claps his hands at your fall." Clapping the hands can be an action of derision and contempt (Job 27:23; 34:37; Lam. 2:15) or of joyful praise and worship (Ps. 47:1; 98:8; Isa. 55:12). Certainly the former is the primary focus here, but the latter is implied as well, for it is Yahweh who humbles Nineveh in the sight of the nations.

The last two lines could be translated "For who has not been overwhelmed / by your continual wickedness" to point out the coincidence of two key terms. Nineveh had "overwhelmed" or "flooded" (*'ābar* [1556]) the world with her aggressive lusts for land and loot. So Yahweh would overwhelm her (1:8) so she would "pass away" (1:12), "completely destroyed" (1:15).

Nineveh overwhelmed the world with her cruel "wickedness" (*rā'â* [2191c]) and had also plotted "evil" against Yahweh. It was for Nineveh's "evil ways" against God and man that Yahweh first sent Jonah to "the great city" (see comments on Jonah 1:2). When the Ninevites repented of their "evil ways," God relented from His "evil" judgment (see comments on Jonah 3:9-10). But, "as a dog returns to its vomit,/so a fool repeats his folly" (Prov. 26:11). Nineveh once again heard the voice of a Hebrew prophet, but this time no compassion or grace was offered.

EPILOGUE

Yahweh is slow to anger—longsuffering. He gives time to consider, time to repent, time to be saved. In the early eighth century B.C., Yahweh moved heaven and earth to save Nineveh and to teach Israel about the nature of His grace and the need for repentance. In the late seventh century, Yahweh again moved heaven and earth to decimate Nineveh and save His people, to teach them of His justice and goodness.

Nahum is a book for our time. As we the living, and the martyrs under the altar (Rev. 6:9), cry out to Yahweh to crush the Hitlers, the Stalins, the Amins and all the others (even those uncomfortably close to home) who crush the peoples of the earth and shake their fists at the God of the universe, we can be strengthened by the message that Yahweh "cares for those who trust him, but with an overwhelming flood he will make an end" of His foes in His time (1:7-8).

APPENDIX: THE USE OF
EXODUS 34:6-7 IN THE SCRIPTURES

Both Jonah and Nahum base the thrust of their books on the content of Exodus 34:6-7, the revelation of the "thirteen attributes" of God according to the Jewish tradition, especially highlighting the attribute of longsuffering. The purpose of this brief appendix is to examine the text of Exodus 34:6-7 in its original setting and then in its various citations throughout the Scriptures.

WITHIN THE BOOK OF EXODUS

EXODUS: THE BOOK OF SALVATION

The book of Exodus contains the most dramatic event of the Hebrew Scriptures, the saving of Israel from slavery in Egypt. Consequently, most scholars and expositors see salvation as the dominant theme of the book. But the exodus event is completed by chapter 14; so how does the rest of the book witness to God's salvation?

The first announcement of that salvation provides us with a clue. Chapters 1 and 2 set up the need for salvation. And because Yahweh "remembered his covenant with Abraham, with Isaac and with Jacob" (2:24), He "[came] down to rescue the Israelites from the hand of the Egyptians and to bring them up out of that land into a good and spacious land, a land flowing with milk and honey" (3:8). Salvation, then, is not just a "bringing out," it is also a "bringing in." Salvation always involves both deliverance and provision. Chapters 1-14 emphasize the deliverance aspect of salvation; 15-40 emphasize the provision.

YAHWEH: THE GOD OF SALVATION

God then revealed His name as "I am who I am" (3:14), which He instructed Moses to pronounce as "Yahweh" (3:15). Summing up the total revelation of Exodus 3, Walther Eichrodt has defined God's unique name "Yahweh" as:

> I am really and truly present,
>   ["I have come down . . . I will be with you"]
> ready to help and to act,
>   ["I have come down to rescue . . . and to bring . . ."]
> as I have always been.
>   ["I am the God of your fathers"][1]

Though Israel's ancestors had been familiar with the name "Yahweh," they had not really "known" God as Yahweh, the God who delivers and provides (6:3). The word "know" here, and throughout the Scriptures (*yādā'* [848]), can have the nuance of intimate personal relationships, as it did when Adam "knew" Eve and they conceived a child (Gen. 4:1, KJV). Israel was enslaved by Egypt because her new Pharaoh did not "know" Joseph (1:8), that is, he had no covenant relation with Joseph and his descendants. However, Yahweh "knew" ("was concerned about") Israel, and this intimacy in covenant relationship prompted His mighty acts of salvation (2:25; 3:7; 4:31).

But Israel needed to know Yahweh as He knew her. Therefore Yahweh announced in 6:7-8:

> I will take you as my own people, and I will be your God. Then you will know that I am Yahweh your God, who brought you out from under the yoke of the Egyptians. And I will bring you to the land I swore with uplifted hand to give to Abraham, to Isaac and to Jacob.

---

1. Walther Eichrodt, *Theology of the Old Testament* (Philadelphia: Westminster, 1961), 1:190.

By mighty acts of judgment and sweet salvation Israel would experience intimacy with God and come to know Him as Yahweh. The Egyptians, too, would know that He was Yahweh, but only because they tasted His judgment (5:2; 7:5, 14; 8:10, 22; 9:14, 29; 11:7; 14:4, 18). This knowledge would not bring intimacy.

SALVATION AS PROVISION

By the end of chapter 14, Israel had come to know Yahweh as the God who delivers. The events of 15 through 17 would provide her with knowledge of Yahweh as the God who provides. The progression and development of this knowledge can be outlined as:

A1. "Yahweh is a Warrior," 15:1-21.
   B1. "Yahweh heals you," 15:22-27.
      C. "Yahweh provides," 16:1-36.
   B2. "Yahweh is among us," 17:1-7.
A2. "Yahweh is my Banner," 17:8-16.

The "A" elements of the outline both deal with war. First, Yahweh fights their battles, for Israel does not yet have the experience upon which to base the faith to do her own fighting. But by the time the people face the Amalekites (17:8-16), they have come to know Yahweh sufficiently to fight their own battles under His direction.

The "B" elements both deal with provision of water. Yahweh heals the water at Marah to demonstrate He can provide for the Israelites' needs in the land, even keeping them free of disease. Yahweh brings water from the rock at Rephidim to demonstrate He is among them. Sandwiched in the middle of the episodes is Yahweh's provision of quail and manna, showing that the same God who delivered them from Egypt can also provide their daily bread.

Notice that each new nuance of the meaning of Yahweh is revealed following Israel's complaints and challenges

(14:11-12; 15:24; 16:2, 7-9, 11; 17:1-3, 7). Only the battle against Amalek has no grumbling. By then, Israel had got into a pattern of "remembering" Yahweh (3:15), that is, acting on the basis of His name.

Notice, too, that Yahweh never judged the people of Israel for this grumbling. They were learning, growing. They had not yet entered the covenant at Sinai. But after that, their rebellions and even their grumblings were severely judged (cf. Ex. 16 with Num. 11).

Thus far, Yahweh had only revealed the salvific side of His name to Israel. Even hearing about this salvation caused Jethro to know Yahweh (18:10-11). And based on knowing the God of salvation, Israel immediately agreed to enter the covenant with Him at Sinai (19:3-8).

YAHWEH: HOLY, INCOMPARABLE, JEALOUS

As the covenant stipulations were revealed, more insights into the divine character emerged, most significantly the holiness and incomparability of Yahweh (20:1-7). Yahweh is the one who saves; therefore no other gods must compete for Israel's affection. Yahweh is a jealous God; He demands exclusive commitment. If not, He will punish the sin of apostasy and idolatry to the third and fourth generation of those who "hate" Him (v. 5). "Hate" here means to forsake commitment or choose not to commit to Yahweh.

On the other hand (v. 6), He maintains His loyal love (*ḥesed* [698a]) to the thousandth generation of those who love (*'āhēb* [29]). The latter word for love is the universal term in the ancient world for covenant loyalty.

All of this sets up the horrifying episode of apostasy with the golden calf (32—34). Israel had agreed to the terms of the covenant (19:8; 24:3, 7). The agreement had been confirmed with blood and a ritual meal in Yahweh's presence (24:8-11). Israel had come to know Yahweh. She had knowingly and willingly entered covenant relation with Him. However, she chose to forsake Yahweh and His covenant and turn to idols!

THE GOLDEN CALF AND THE LONGSUFFERING OF YAHWEH

The well-known story of the golden calf (32—34) needs no repeating in detail. But several elements should be noted. First, Moses shattered the tablets of the law, signifying the breaking of the covenant (32:19). Second, the wicked among the people were judicially killed by the Levites (32:28) and the Lord (32:35). Third, though Yahweh had every right to abandon Israel, Moses argued on the basis of Yahweh's name and His covenant with the fathers that Yahweh relent from destroying (32:11-13) or abandoning (33:15-16) the people. Yahweh did relent (see comments on Jonah 3:10), though His holiness and exclusiveness were vindicated by judgments.

YAHWEH: THE GOD OF LONGSUFFERING

Moses then a vision of God's glory (33:18). Yahweh agreed, stating He would display His glory both by proclaiming His own name and by allowing Moses to view the back parts of His glory (33:19-23).

Yahweh commanded Moses to prepare two new tablets, a concrete sign that forgiveness had taken place. The next day, Moses once again ascended the mountain and Yahweh proclaimed His name, revealing the essence of His character that allows him to forgive sin, yet maintain His holiness and justice (34:6-7):

> Yahweh, Yahweh, the compassionate and gracious God, slow to anger, abounding in love and faithfulness, maintaining love to thousands, and forgiving wickedness, rebellion and sin. Yet he does not leave the guilty unpunished; he punishes the children and their children for the sin of the fathers to the third and fourth generation.

"Yahweh, Yahweh." By twice pronouncing His name, Yahweh doubly emphasizes the essential characteristics this name reveals: presence, salvation, provision, and constancy. This is the standard way of expressing a superlative in

Hebrew, as in the "holy of holies" indicating the holiest of all holy places, the "Lord of lords" indicating the most sovereign of all sovereigns, even "I am who I am" (3:14).

"The compassionate and gracious God." This line states the tone of the whole proclamation. Yahweh is God (*'ēl* [93a]), as opposed to man. But the kind of God He is is expressed by the terms that follow. "Compassion" (*raḥûm* [2146c]), is related to the word for "womb," and aptly describes the "deep love (usually of a 'superior' for an 'inferior') rooted in some 'natural' bond" (TWOT, p. 841). It can also imply that this compassion is being extended to one who does not deserve it (Ps. 78:37-38). "Gracious" (*ḥannûn* [694d]) is a close synonym of "compassion." These terms are coupled ten other times (2 Chron. 30:9; Neh. 9:17, 31; Ps. 86:15; 103:8; 111:4; 112:4; 145:8; Joel 2:13; Jonah 4:2), seven of which (at least) are direct quotations of this verse. (See also 33:19.)

"Slow to anger" (*'ārēk* [162b] and *'ap* [133a]). Here is the King James Version's "longsuffering," a fine translation, for it emphasizes that Yahweh withholds His judgment on sin, "suffering long" or patiently enduring as He gives sinners the opportunity to repent. But as the following lines confirm, longsuffering is both gracious and judgmental. For though the wicked are given time to repent and receive grace instead of anger, those who do not turn have had time to heap up even more judgment for themselves (cf. Matt. 11:20-24).

"Abounding in love and faithfulness." "Love" is the strong word *ḥesed* (698a), which combines the ideas of affection and absolute loyalty, thus is often rendered "loyal love" or "unfailing love." "Faithfulness" (*'ĕmet* [116k]), by itself is often translated "truth" or "true" (Ps. 119:43, 142, 151, 160). These words appear as a pair more than a dozen times in Scripture (e.g., Gen. 32:10; Ps. 25:10; 26:3; 115:1; Isa. 16:5). Together they emphasize the dependability of God's love.

"Maintaining love to thousands." "Love" here is also *ḥesed*. "Thousands" recalls 20:6, "showing love to thou-

sands who love me and keep my commandments." Paralleling 20:5, and here the end of verse 7, "thousands" probably
means "the thousandth generation." Though God's judgment extends to the third and fourth generation, His loyal
love is perpetuated for a thousand.

"Forgiving wickedness, rebellion and sin." "Forgiving"
(*nāśā'* [1421]) often communicates the concrete idea of picking up and carrying away (Gen. 7:17; Ex. 10:19). It is significantly used of the bearing of sin by the Suffering Servant
of Isaiah 53 (vv. 4, 12; cf. John 1:29). Yahweh can take away
the sin of those who love Him and express that love in obedience.

The words for sin represent a broad vocabulary of strong
terminology. "Wickedness" (*'āwōn* [1577a]) denotes both the
act of sin and the punishment for sin (Ex. 20:5; 34:7*b*).
"Rebellion" (*pesha'* [1846a]) is a term used in biblical and
secular literature of covenant violation between nations
(1 Kings 12:19; 2 Kings 1:1; 3:5, 7), thus of violation of
Yahweh's covenant (Isa. 1:2, 28; Hos. 8:1). "Sin" (*haṭṭā'â*
[638c]) is the standard word for the category of unright
behavior, "missing the mark or way" that God has established (cf. Judg. 20:16). Because of His *ḥesed,* His love for
those who love Him, Yahweh will take away the punishment
for covenant rebellion or any kind of sin that can be com-
mitted.

"Yet he does not leave the guilty unpunished." This can be
rendered, "But by no means does He declare all to be innocent!" The verb "leave unpunished" (*nāqâ* [1412]) is
repeated twice, again for emphasis. Yahweh is not sentimen-
tal in His love. He "loves" (forgives) those who love Him; He
"hates" (justly judges) those who hate Him.

"He punishes the children for the sin of the fathers."
"Sin" is the same as "wickedness" above. "Punish"
translates a word (*pāqad* [1802]) with a broad range of meaning, from "number" to "reckon" to "take action to cause a
considerable change in the circumstances of the subordinate,

whether for better or for worse" (TWOT, p. 731). It is used here with the latter, negative meaning.

Although the concept of "punishing the children for the sin of the fathers to the third and fourth generation" may seem unfair, note the strong contrast to the thousand generations who receive His love. (This principle is, however, done away with in the New Covenant, "everyone will die for his own sin," Jeremiah 31:29-30).

It is clear that these attributes of God, especially as they are described in a statement made by Yahweh himself, are of extreme significance to the covenant relationship of Yahweh and His people. We are not surprised, then, to find this passage reiterated in at least nine important passages. The following are brief descriptions of the use of Exodus 34:6-7 in the rest of the Scriptures, according to an approximately chronological order.

Numbers 14:17-19

The apostasy with the golden calf was Israel's first great sin. Refusing to enter the Land (Num. 13—14) was the second. Because the people threatened to break with their leaders and return to Egypt (14:2-4), Yahweh again had the right to break with them (14:11-12).

Again, Moses pleaded with Yahweh on the basis of His name and the covenant (14:13-19). But now, instead of calling on the covenant with the fathers (Ex. 32:13), he called on the covenant at Sinai by quoting Exodus 34:6-7 with slight omissions of vocabulary but no loss of meaning. He stressed the greatness of Yahweh's *hesed* as the basis of forgiving His people.

Yahweh does forgive. "Yet he does not leave the guilty unpunished"; He punished the entire generation of those over 40 who refused to enter the land of Canaan. Forgiveness does not imply that there will be no consequences of the wrong actions. Yahweh was faithful to His people in forgiving their sin, but He was faithful to His own character in not allowing them to go unpunished.

PSALM 86:5, 15

Psalm 86 is, according to its title, a psalm of David. It is a Psalm of Lament,[2] a petition requesting the salvation of God. David was in distress, specifically under the attack of arrogant and ruthless men (v. 14). He requests Yahweh to save him because he has maintained devotion to Yahweh. He is "devoted" (a cognate of *ḥesed*), and needs Yahweh's "devotion" ("love," *ḥesed*; 5, 13, 15).

The central reference to Yahweh's *ḥesed* contains, word for word, Exodus 34:6, except that "Yahweh" has been replaced by "Lord" (*'adōnāy* [27b]), emphasizing David's position as servant. David only quotes verse 6, for he only requests Yahweh's compassionate salvation and merciful grace. He does not need his sin to be forgiven, nor does he wish judgment on others (other than the allusion in v. 17a), so he does not quote verse 7.

Note that David prays for Yahweh's help on the basis of His past faithfulness to both David (vv. 13, 17b) and Israel (v. 15). This is similar to Jonah's prayer, where he praises Yahweh for *ḥesed* shown to him (2:8) and recognizes his *ḥesed* to Israel as well (4:2).

PSALM 103:8

Psalm 103 also purports to be a psalm of David. But now, instead of an individual's prayer for salvation, it is a Psalm of Descriptive Praise.[3] It dwells on the amazing forgiveness of Yahweh from verse 3 on. And once again, in the center of the Psalm (8), David quotes Exodus 34:6 as the greatest credal expression of Yahweh's forgiveness.

He also alludes to 34:7, by citing all three words for sin in

2. Claus Westermann, *Praise and Lament in the Psalms,* pp. 64ff.
3. Westermann, pp. 116ff.

verses 10 and 12. And he makes clear who can expect Yahweh's *hesed* in verses 11, 17, and 18: those who fear Him (cf. Jon. 1:9, 16), keep His covenant, and obey His precepts (cf. Ex. 20:6).

This is a psalm like Jonah's, a psalm praising Yahweh for His salvation. But not just salvation from distress, salvation from sin.

PSALM 145:8

Psalm 145 is also a Psalm of Descriptive Praise by David. This psalm praises Yahweh more generally in relation to His compassionate goodness, that is, it does not concentrate on goodness as expressed in forgiveness.

This psalm differs from the others in structure in that it is an acrostic psalm, that is, each verse begins with the successive letter of the Hebrew alphabet. And as the psalmist came to verse 8 and the Hebrew letter *ḥet*, what better expression of his "abundant goodness" than the forgiveness expressed at the apostasy with the golden calf. Interestingly, the words "gracious" and "love" both begin with this letter.

As in the other Psalms, only Exodus 34:6 is quoted. But fear and obedience are again in view in verses 18-20, with all the standard vocabulary. Also in view in these verses, and new in application, is the notion that Yahweh's compassion extends to *all* that He has made. This opens the door, at least, for the blatant application made of Exodus 34:6-7 in Jonah to the Gentiles.

JOEL 2:13

The book of Joel is notoriously difficult to date, estimates ranging from the days of Elijah to the days of Ezra. Almost all scholars, however, agree that the book predated Jonah and was used by him.

Joel is apparently the first prophet to use Exodus 34:6 to call Israel back into right relation to Yahweh. David in Psalm

86 had used it for himself, and in Psalm 103 saw it as under-girding all of Yahweh's forgiving ways. But Joel, after calling Israel to return to Yahweh wholeheartedly, "with fasting and weeping and mourning" (2:12), quotes Exodus 34:6 as witnessing to the potential of Yahweh's turning back to them.

Joel further reinforces this understanding with Exodus 32:12 and 14, that Yahweh "relents from sending calamity." In Exodus 20:5 and 34:14, Yahweh stated that He is a "jealous God." Israel had turned her attention away from the worship of Yahweh and maintenance of the Temple. So Yahweh brought a locust plague to devastate the land so the people would experience what it was like not to have their food and drink offerings.

But if they turned, "Who knows but that he may turn and have pity/and leave behind a blessing—/grain offerings and drink offerings/for Yahweh your God" (2:14). This would happen when the jealous God could once again be "jealous for his land/and take pity on his people" (2:18).

Joel contributes to the understanding of Exodus 34:6 that Yahweh can be approached on the basis of His compassion even while under judgment, though He gives no guarantee of a mechanical relationship between repentance and forgiveness with his "Who knows?" of 2:14.

JONAH 4:2

As developed in the commentary, the entire book of Jonah addresses the salvation of Yahweh, not just for Israel but also for the whole world. It clearly teaches in 4:2 that Jonah expected that Yahweh was required to save the Ninevites because they had turned to Him in repentance. But it also teaches that Jonah and his readers did not want the Gentiles to share in Yahweh's compassion.

Jonah makes explicit what Psalm 145 stated implicitly, that Yahweh is compassionate toward all He has made. In a fascinating parallel, Psalms 111 and 112 both use "gracious and compassionate" as a couplet in alphabetic psalms of Declarative Praise. But 111 speaks of Yahweh, 112 speaks of the *individual* who expresses these attributes. Jonah agreed with Psalm 111, but could not find it in his heart to apply 112.

NAHUM 1:3

As mentioned in the commentary, the use of Exodus 34:6-7 in Nahum 1:3 is debatable, but is a strong option. Verse 3 quotes 34:6 that "Yahweh is slow to anger," but surprisingly changes "great in love and faithfulness" to "great in power." Chapter 34, verse 7 is then directly cited, "he will not leave the guilty unpunished."

Longsuffering is gracious in that those who do respond rightly are saved. In Jonah the gracious side of Yahweh's longsuffering is seen, resulting in the salvation of the sailors, the Ninevites, and the potential salvation of Jonah. That is why Jonah limited his citation to 34:6. However, longsuffering is also *judgmental* in that those who do not respond have added to their sin and thus have greatly increased their judgment. In Nahum this judgmental side of longsuffering is seen, resulting in the ultimate destruction of unrepentant Nineveh. That is why Nahum altered his citation of 34:6 and continued to 34:7.

As Jonah had boldly applied 34:6 to the nations, so Nahum applied 34:7. The guilt of Nineveh finally caught up to her.

NEHEMIAH 9:17

In a petition for God's forgiveness, Nehemiah cites Exodus 34:6 and the whole episode involving the golden calf as an example of past compassion. This prayer followed the Israelites' "fasting and wearing sackcloth" (9:1) after the pattern of Joel, and "confessing their sins and the wickedness of their fathers" (9:2), two of the three words from Exodus 34:7.

In this model prayer, as in David's of Psalm 86, Exodus

34:6-7 is fundamental to the approach to Yahweh according to His character and His past dealings. In verse 17, Nehemiah adds the phrase "you are a forgiving God," recalling the vocabulary of Exodus 34:9, repeated in Numbers 14:19-20; Psalm 86:5 and 103:3.

JOHN 1:14

Is it any wonder, then, that in the greatest expression of the forgiveness of Yahweh, the coming of Jesus as the Savior of the world, Exodus 34:6-7 should once again be in view. For when Jesus displayed His glory, it was "full of grace and truth," that is "abounding in love and faithfulness."

Jesus came, because of the Father's love and compassion, to take away the sins of the world (John 1:29; 3:16). He commanded those who loved Him to keep His commandments (14:15) and continue to show Him loyal love (15:9-11). But He also came to judge those who rejected Him (9:39, 41).

The compassionate and gracious God who forgave Israel in the wilderness, who forgave David, who forgave Israel in the days of Joel, who forgave Jonah and Nineveh, continues to offer forgiveness to all who turn to him in love, fear, and obedience through Jesus the Messiah. But the jealous God who executed a generation in the wilderness, who sent a nation into exile, and who tore down godless kingdoms continues to hate those who hate Him. The side of God each individual deals with depends on the decision to love or hate, to fear or mock, to serve God or serve self. "But as for me and my household, we will serve Yahweh" (Josh. 24:15).

BIBLIOGRAPHY

Alcorn, Wallace A. "Jonah, Book of." In *Wycliffe Bible Encyclopedia,* 1:944-47. Edited by Charles F. Pfeiffer et al. Chicago: Moody, 1975.

    A well-written, conservative introduction.

Allen, Leslie C. *The Books of Joel, Obadiah, Jonah and Micah.* New International Commentary on the Old Testament. Grand Rapids: Eerdmans, 1976.

    Perhaps the best commentary on Jonah. Evangelical, though not fundamentalist. Dates Jonah after the exile and allows the author literary freedom with history.

Archer, Gleason L. *A Survey of Old Testament Introduction.* Rev. ed. Chicago: Moody, 1974.

    Very conservative introduction. Thoroughly discusses historical and linguistic problems.

Bewer, Julius A. "A Commentary on Jonah." In *A Critical and Exegetical Commentary on Haggai, Zechariah, Malachi and Jonah.* Edinburgh: T. & T. Clark, 1912.

    The classic liberal, critical commentary. Thorough, though dated, treatment. Incredulous attitude toward historicity.

Buttrick, George A., ed. *Interpreter's Dictionary of the Bible.* Nashville: Abingdon, 1962.

Childs, Brevard S. *Introduction to the Old Testament as Scripture.* Philadelphia: Fortress, 1979.

    Thorough treatment of the theological message of Jonah and Nahum as they exist in canon. Excellent bibliographies.

Cohen, A., ed. *The Twelve Prophets.* Soncino Books of the Bible. London: Soncino, 1948.

Fine conservative Jewish commentary.

Douglas, J. D., ed. *New Bible Dictionary.* Rev. ed. Wheaton, Ill.: Tyndale, 1982.

Griffiths, Michael C. "Jonah." In *The New Layman's Bible Commentary,* pp. 975-87. Edited by G. C. D. Howley et al. Grand Rapids: Zondervan, 1979.

Excellent short treatment in a fine one-volume whole Bible commentary. Well written and documented.

Harris, R. Laird et al., eds. *Theological Wordbook of the Old Testament* Chicago: Moody, 1980. Referred to in text as TWOT.

Hertz, J. H. *The Pentateuch and Haftorahs.* 2d ed. London: Soncino, 1960.

Another fine, brief Jewish treatment on Jonah, hidden in a commentary on the books of Moses (pp. 964-71).

Keil, C. F. "Minor Prophets." In *Commentary on the OT.* Reprint. Grand Rapids: Eerdmans, 1975.

A classic conservative treatment. Thorough, though dated.

Kittel, Gerhard, and Gerhard Friedrich, eds. *Theological Dictionary of the New Testament.* Grand Rapids: Eerdmans, 1964-1976.

Landes, G. M. "Jonah, Book of." In *The Interpreter's Dictionary of the Bible,* supplementary volume. 5:488-91. Edited by George A. Buttrick. Nashville: Abingdon, 1976.
———. "The Kerygma of the Book of Jonah." *Interpretation* 21 (1967): 3:31.

Both articles argue eloquently for the unity of Jonah, and a date just before the fall of Judah. "Kerygma" is especially valuable for detailed structural analysis.

Maier, Walter A. *The Book of Nahum.* 1959. Reprint. Grand Rapids: Baker, 1980.

The classic conservative work on Nahum. Thorough historical, textual, and linguistic discussion.

Neil, W. "Jonah, Book of." In *The Interpreter's Dictionary of the Bible,* 2:964-67. Edited by George A Buttrick. Nashville: Abingdon, 1962.

Presents the modern liberal understanding of the book.

Robinson, D. W. B. "Jonah." In *The New Bible Commentary: Revised*. Edited by Donald Guthrie et al. Grand Rapids: Eerdmans, 1970.

Another fine brief treatment in a standard one-volume commentary.

Smith, George Adam. "The Book of the Twelve Prophets." In *The Expositor's Bible,* vol. 4. Reprint. Grand Rapids: Eerdmans, 1956.

An eloquently written, often quoted treatment of Jonah from the allegorical perspective. Good spiritual insights.

Smith, John Merlin Powis. "A Commentary on Nahum." In *A Critical and Exegetical Commentary on Micah, Zephaniah, Nahum, Habakkuk, Obadiah and Joel*. Edinburgh: T. & T. Clark, 1911.

The standard liberal work. Very thorough, though dated, in introduction and exegesis.

Smith, Ralph L. *Micah-Malachi*. Word Biblical Commentary. Waco, Tex.: Word, 1984.

The most recent and up-to-date commentary. Thorough textual, literary, and historical treatment. Excellent bibliographies. Valuable for students and scholars.

Stuart, Douglas. *Hosea-Jonah*. Word Biblical Commentary. Waco, Tex.: Word, 1984.

This was not published in time to use in preparing this commentary, but it will no doubt be very thorough and up-to-date. Valuable for students and scholars.

Taylor, Charles L. "The Book of Nahum." In *The Interpreter's Bible,* vol. 6, pp. 953-69. Nashville: Abingdon, 1956.

Brief but thorough critical commentary with a full translation of the text, showing the standard reworking of the acrostic of 1:2-9 and marking alleged insertions with brackets.

Thomas, D. W., ed. *Documents from Old Testament Times.* New York: Harper & Row, 1961.

von Rad, Gerhard. *Old Testament Theology.* New York: Harper & Row, 1962.

   This is a radically liberal but extremely insightful treatment of OT theology, especially of the prophets.

Walton, John. *Jonah.* Bible Study Commentary. Grand Rapids: Zondervan, 1982.

   A fine recent treatment. Especially good for historical and linguistic information.

Westermann, Claus. *Praise and Lament in the Psalms.* Atlanta: John Knox, 1981.

   Significant for the analysis of Jonah 2 and praise in general.

Moody Press, a ministry of the Moody Bible Institute, is designed for education, evangelization, and edification. If we may assist you in knowing more about Christ and the Christian life, please write us without obligation: Moody Press, c/o MLM, Chicago, Illinois 60610.